Dancing with the Tiger

A Coppin State University Sundance Reader

Mark Connelly, Joseph Trimmer & Frederick Douglass

D1304366

CENGAGE
Learning™

Australia • Brazil • Japan • Korea • Mexico • Singapore • Spain • United Kingdom • United States

CENGAGE
Learning™

Dancing with the Tiger

Mark Connelly, Joseph Trimmer
& Frederick Douglass

Executive Editors:
Michele Baird

Maureen Staudt

Michael Stranz

Project Development Manager:
Linda deStefano

Senior Marketing Coordinators:
Sara Mercurio

Lindsay Shapiro

Senior Production /
Manufacturing Manager:
Donna M. Brown

PreMedia Services Supervisor:
Rebecca A. Walker

Rights & Permissions Specialist:
Kalina Hintz

Cover Image:
Getty Images*

* Unless otherwise noted, all
cover images used by Custom
Solutions, a part of Cengage
Learning, have been supplied
courtesy of Getty Images with
the exception of the Earthview
cover image, which has been
supplied by the National
Aeronautics and Space
Administration (NASA).

For product information and
technology assistance, contact us at **Cengage Learning
Customer & Sales Support, 1-800-354-9706**

For permission to use material from this text or product,
submit all requests online at **cengage.com/permissions**
Further permissions questions can be emailed to
permissionrequest@cengage.com

ISBN-13:   978-1-4240-4913-4

ISBN-10:   1-4240-4913-X

Cengage Learning
5191 Natorp Boulevard
Mason, Ohio 45040
USA

Cengage Learning is a leading provider of customized learning
solutions with office locations around the globe, including
Singapore, the United Kingdom, Australia, Mexico, Brazil, and Japan.
Locate your local office at: **international.cengage.com/region**

Cengage Learning products are represented in Canada by
Nelson Education, Ltd.

For your lifelong learning solutions, visit **custom.cengage.com**

Visit our corporate website at **cengage.com**

Printed in the United States of America

Acknowledgements

The content of this text has been adapted from the following product(s):

Description: Cisneros, Sandra, Only Daughter
ISBN-10: (1-428-25587-7)
ISBN-13: ()

Process: Giovanni, Nikki, Campus Racism 101
ISBN-10: (1-428-25850-7)
ISBN-13: ()

Narrative: Gansberg, Martin, Thirty-Eight Who Saw Murder Didn't Call the Police
ISBN-10: (1-428-25569-9)
ISBN-13: ()

Definition: Truth, Sojourner, Ain't I a Woman?
ISBN-10: (1-428-25627-X)
ISBN-13: ()

War on Terrorism: Friedman, Thomas, Because We Could
ISBN-10: (1-428-25660-1)
ISBN-13: ()

Argument/Persuasion: Sherry, Mary, In Praise of the "F" Word
ISBN-10: (1-428-26042-0)
ISBN-13: ()

Rhetoric: Developing a Thesis
ISBN-10: (1-428-25195-2)
ISBN-13: ()

Narrative: Angelou, Maya, Champion of the World
ISBN-10: (1-428-25574-5)
ISBN-13: ()

War on Terrorism: Karim, A. Tariq, Terrorism: Addressing Its Root Causes

ISBN-10: (1-428-25665-2)
ISBN-13: ()

Islam and the West: Mohamad, Mahathir bin, Terrorism and Islam: Maintaining Our Faith
ISBN-10: (1-428-25871-X)
ISBN-13: ()

Introduction: Learning to Read
ISBN-10: ()
ISBN-13: ()

Comparison/Contrast: Soto, Gary, Like Mexicans
ISBN-10: (1-428-25805-1)
ISBN-13: ()

Analysis: Raspberry, William, The Handicap of Definition
ISBN-10: (1-428-25825-6)
ISBN-13: ()

Process: Elbow, Peter, Desperation Writing
ISBN-10: (1-428-26014-5)
ISBN-13: ()

Process: Keillor, Garrison, How to Write a Letter
ISBN-10: (1-428-25852-3)
ISBN-13: ()

Argument/Persuasion: Hentoff, Nat, Should This Student have Been Expelled?
ISBN-10: (1-428-26049-8)
ISBN-13: ()

Narrative: Malcom X, Prison Studies
ISBN-10: (1-428-25567-2)
ISBN-13: ()

Table Of Contents

Introduction: Learning to Read (the Prerequisite to Learning to Write)

"If you give a [slave] an inch, he will take an ell. Learning will spoil the best [slave] in the world. He should know nothing about the will of his master, and learn to obey it. If you teach him how to read, he will want to know how to write, and this accomplished, he will be running away with himself."

−Frederick Douglass

"Follow the Drinking Gourd."

−Anonymous

"All Writing is Rewriting."

−Anonymous

Welcome to the *Dancing with the Tiger*, the 1st edition of Coppin State University's

customized reader for English 101 and 102. These fifteen essays have been selected to assist you

in learning *to read* as every writer should: slowly, carefully, and thoughtfully.

You may be wondering, "If I'm taking a course in writing, why am I expected to read?"

The answer is easy. As Frederick Douglass (1818-1895) writes in his autobiography, *The*

Narrative of the Life of Frederick Douglass, reading opens up a new world. Slaves were

forbidden to read, not just because it would distract them from the backbreaking tedium of

fieldwork, but because an educated slave was no longer a slave, but a free man (or woman) in the

making. Like Douglass, he would begin to learn new words, like "abolition."

Like freedom, reading is an end in itself; but, it is also a precious skill for all apprentice

writers. Studies confirm that there is a close connection between being able to read well and

being able to write effectively. In fact, learning to write is only possible when we learn to read *our own writing* with a writer's eye – to see *possibilities* that a less skilled writer would never spot. And, as Frederick Douglass knew, once you have learned how to write, you have mastered a powerful art. Words will open doors for you.

Learning to read more skillfully, so that we can write more effectively, involves developing the imagination. No first draft lives up to its potential. In fact, one of the best-concealed tricks of the writer's trade is that no writer, not even the best, achieves a mastery of his or her subject in the first draft. Ernest Hemingway (1899-1961), one of the greatest of American novelists, revised the conclusion to *Farewell to Arms* 43 times. Likewise, the essays contained in this volume went through many drafts to achieve the clarity, coherence, and concision of the final versions you are reading here.

If we can learn to imitate this process –to read our own early drafts with critical sympathy – we will become better writers. As we read and rewrite our own work, moving through the stages of redrafting, revising, and editing, we will see that we can word things more effectively than we did in our first clumsy attempts.

Here is a magic trick. Before you continue reading this introduction, do a little exercise.

First, turn to the table of contents of *Dancing With the Tiger*. Look over the titles of the essays and pick one that you'd like to read. But before you start reading, take out a piece of paper and a pen or pencil. I like a pencil, but if you prefer pen, use that instead.

As you read, stop at intervals to write. In fact, after you've chosen your essay to read, answer the first set of questions, using at least 4-6 sentences:

1) Why did you pick this essay? What was it about the title, or your own experience, that attracted you to it even before you started reading?

Then read the first paragraph of the essay and answer questions #2 and #3:

2) What do you think the thesis (main idea) is?

3) What is your response to the first paragraph?

Notice that "what is your response?" is an open question, one that invites you to be creative and thoughtful. There is no right or wrong answer, only an undeveloped or a well-developed one. At a later stage in the composition process, you may want to consider how coherent your paragraphs are, how carefully you have edited each sentence, how well you have phrased your thoughts, or how interesting your responses might be for your readers. But don't worry about that right now. For now, just enjoy the writing, explore the topic, and satisfy yourself.

Finally, finish reading the essay, and answer these two final sets of questions:

4) Looking back at your answer to question #2, what arguments or evidence does the writer use to develop his or her thesis?

5) What is your response to the entire essay? Has your perspective on the subject changed since you started reading or completed the first paragraph? How? What have you learned? What has changed *in you* through reading?

Write at least five sentences on the first question, and at least ten on the second set. You're done.

There, that wasn't so difficult, was it? You just generated the draft of a response essay. Believe it or not, you used all the basic "moves" needed for a successful essay of this kind. What you just did, in fact, is a model for how you should approach all assignments that require you to write in response to a reading. Notice that such a writing assignment invariably has two basic elements to it:

1) You need to be able to accurately assess the contents of the reading. That means, in your own words, to paraphrase or summarize what the article is saying, including both thesis (main idea) and support (evidence or reasons).

2) You need to have *a response* to what you are reading.

Notice, also, that *responding* requires you to step forward and take some risks as a writer. You can't hide behind your sources, and you *shouldn't* let what anyone else has said be last word on your subject. In fact, the word "essay" is derived from the French verb, *essayer,* which means to "try" or "attempt." The inventor of the essay, the French philosopher Michel De Montaigne (1533-1592), said in his *Les Essaies*, "I quote others only in order to express myself more fully." Make that your motto and you will never go wrong in your use of sources.

When you submit an essay for a grade, it should be the best work that you can do. But tomorrow, you will reread that same essay and see you could have done something better – more insightful, more entertaining, or more stylish. When that happens, you know that you are really on board the freedom train. Good luck!

– Roger Stritmatter, PhD

Special thanks to Rev. Elaine Sykes, Mr. Paul Gass, and Ms. Zenia Jenkins, for their revision suggestions.

Postscript

Framing responses to your reading can be a challenge. For some assistance, please see appendix A, which gives you a set of templates for wording summaries, quotations, and responses.

For additional information on Frederick Douglass and his autobiography, consult your online resources.

2

PETER ELBOW

Peter Elbow (1935–) was educated at Williams College, Brandeis, Harvard, and Oxford. A noted director of college writing programs, Elbow started a highly acclaimed "Workshop in Language and Thinking" at Bard College. He has published numerous articles about writing and several books, including Writing without Teachers *(1973) and* Writing with Power *(1981).*

Desperation Writing

BEFORE YOU READ: *In this section from* Writing without Teachers, *Peter Elbow offers advice to students writing under stress. Facing deadlines, many students feel almost paralyzed, unable to even start an assignment. Elbow presents his recommendations in the form of a process.*

TIPS FOR READING: *Think of times when you have had trouble writing because you could not organize your ideas. Elbow offers suggestions such as writing single ideas on small pieces of paper or 3 × 5 cards that you can shuffle or rearrange to discover new relationships between them. This technique may help you with complicated assignments like research papers when you have to juggle opinions, facts, and ideas from a number of sources.*

Words to Know:

recurring	repeating
coherent	clear
hindrance	block
out of commission	not working
incapable	unable
perception	understanding
assertion	statement
comatose	passed out, exhausted
mulling	think over
invariably	always
exert	use
intuition	instinct
deploy	spread out, use
subsidiary	secondary, minor
configuration	pattern or design
associative	dependent on association or relationships

metaphor	figure of speech
refrain	hold back
intrudes	enters without being welcome

1   I know I am not alone in my recurring twinges of panic that I won't be able to write something when I need to, I won't be able to produce coherent speech or thought. And that lingering doubt is a great hindrance to writing. It's a constant fog or static that clouds the mind. I never got out of its clutches till I discovered that it was possible to write something—not something great or pleasing but at least something usable, workable—when my mind is out of commission. The trick is that you have to do all your cooking out on the table: Your mind is incapable of doing any inside. It means using symbols and pieces of paper not as a crutch but as a wheelchair.

2   The first thing is to admit your condition: Because of some mood or event or whatever, your mind is incapable of anything that could be called thought. It can put out a babbling kind of speech utterance, it can put a simple feeling, perception or sort-of-thought into understandable (though terrible) words. But it is incapable of considering anything in relation to anything else. The moment you try to hold that thought or feeling up against some other to see the relationship, you simply lose the picture—you get nothing but buzzing lines or waving colors.

3   So admit this. Avoid anything more than one feeling, perception, or thought. Simply write as much as possible. Try simply to steer your mind in the direction or general vicinity of the thing you are trying to write about and start writing and keep writing.

4   Just write and keep writing. (Probably best to write on only one side of the paper in case you should want to cut parts out with scissors—but you probably won't.) Just write and keep writing. It will probably come in waves. After a flurry, stop and take a brief rest. But don't stop too long. Don't think about what you are writing or what you have written or else you will overload the circuit again. Keep writing as though you are drugged or drunk. Keep doing this till you feel you have a lot of material that might be useful; or, if necessary, till you can't stand it any more—even if you doubt that there's anything useful there.

5   Then take a pad of little pieces of paper—or perhaps 3 × 5 cards—and simply start at the beginning of what you were writing, and as you read over what you wrote, every time you come to any thought, feeling, perception, or image that could be gathered up into one sentence or one assertion, do so and write it by itself on a little sheet of paper. In short, you are trying to turn, say, ten or twenty pages of wandering mush into twenty or thirty hard

little crab apples. Sometimes there won't be many on a page. But if it seems to you that there are none on a page, you are making a serious error—the same serious error that put you in this comatose state to start with. You are mistaking lousy, stupid, second-rate, wrong, childish, foolish, worthless ideas for no ideas at all. Your job is not to pick out *good* ideas but to pick out ideas. As long as you were conscious, your words will be full of things that could be called feelings, utterances, ideas—things that can be squeezed into one simple sentence. This is your job. Don't ask for too much.

6   After you have done this, take those little slips or cards, read through them a number of times—not struggling with them, simply wandering and mulling through them; perhaps shifting them around and looking through in various sequences. In a sense these are cards you are playing solitaire with, and the rules of this particular game permit shuffling the unused pile.

7   The goal of this procedure with the cards is to get them to distribute themselves in two or three or ten or fifteen different piles on your desk. You can get them to do this almost by themselves if you simply keep reading through them in different orders; certain cards will begin to feel like they go with other cards. I emphasize this passive, thoughtless mode because I want to talk about desperation writing in its pure state. In practice, almost invariably at some point in the procedure, your sanity begins to return. It is often at this point. You actually are moved to have thoughts or—and the difference between active and passive is crucial here—to *exert* thought; to hold two cards together and *build* or *assert* a relationship. It is a matter of bringing energy to bear.

8   So you may start to be able to do something active with these cards, and begin actually to think. But if not, just allow the cards to find their own piles with each other by feel, by drift, by intuition, by mindlessness.

9   You have now engaged in the two main activities that will permit you to get something cooked out on the table rather than in your brain: writing out into messy words, summing up into single assertions, and even sensing relationships between assertions. You can simply continue to deploy these two activities.

10   If, for example, after the first round of writing, assertion-making, and pile-making, your piles feel as though they are useful and satisfactory for what you are writing—paragraphs or sections or trains of thought—then you can carry on from there. See if you can gather each pile up into a single assertion. When you can, then put the subsidiary assertions of that pile into their best order to fit with that single unifying one. If you *can't* get the pile into one assertion, then take the pile as the basis for doing some more writing out into words. In the course of this writing, you may produce for

yourself the single unifying assertion you were looking for; or you may have to go through the cycle of turning the writing into assertions and piles and so forth. Perhaps more than once. The pile may turn out to want to be two or more piles itself; or it may want to become part of a pile you already have. This is natural. This kind of meshing into one configuration, then coming apart, then coming together and meshing into a different configuration— this is growing and cooking. It makes a terrible mess, but if you can't do it in your head, you have to put up with a cluttered desk and a lot of confusion.

11   If, on the other hand, all that writing *didn't* have useful material in it, it means that your writing wasn't loose, drifting, quirky, jerky, associative enough. This time try especially to let things simply remind you of things that are seemingly crazy or unrelated. Follow these odd associations. Make as many metaphors as you can—be as nutty as possible—and explore the metaphors themselves—open them out. You may have all your energy tied up in some area of your experience that you are leaving out. Don't refrain from writing about whatever else is on your mind: how you feel at the moment, what you are losing your mind over, randomness that intrudes itself on your consciousness, the pattern on the wallpaper, what those people you see out the window have on their minds—though keep coming back to the whateveritis you are supposed to be writing about. Treat it, in short, like ten-minute writing exercises. Your best perceptions and thoughts are always going to be tied up in whatever is really occupying you, and that is also where your energy is. You may end up writing a love poem—or a hate poem—in one of those little piles while the other piles will finally turn into a lab report on data processing or whatever you have to write about. But you couldn't, in your present state of having your head shot off, have written that report without also writing the poem. And the report will have some of the juice of the poem in it and vice versa.

Understanding Meaning

1. What is Elbow's purpose?
2. What problems does Elbow want to help students to overcome?
3. Do you find this advice helpful? Would you use it?
4. *CRITICAL THINKING.* What does Elbow's essay reveal to you about the writing process? Why is it important to see writing as a process and not merely a product?

Evaluating Strategy

1. Does the opening adequately demonstrate the need for this process?
2. Are the stages or steps clearly defined?
3. How does Elbow signal transitions?

Appreciating Language

1. Elbow writes of ideas that are "lousy" and "stupid" but still have value. What is he trying to indicate to students with these word choices?
2. Judging by the language, what audience, what type of student, is this essay targeted to?

Writing Suggestions

1. Experiment with the freewriting process Elbow describes. Select a topic, and write nonstop for at least ten minutes. Afterward underline the ideas you came up with while writing.
2. *COLLABORATIVE WRITING.* Talk about writing with a group of students. Discuss working methods. Take notes on the tips you feel are helpful. Work with others to craft these tips into a process essay.

3

GARRISON KEILLOR

Almost single-handedly, Garrison Keillor (1942–) revived the radio variety show in an era of films and television. In A Prairie Home Companion, *which is broadcast on National Public Radio every Saturday night, Keillor popularized the mythical community of Lake Wobegon. His homespun humor and whimsical social commentary can also be found in such books as* Happy to Be Here *(1982),* Lake Wobegon Days *(1985),* Leaving Home: A Collection of Lake Wobegon Stories *(1987),* We Are Still Married *(1989),* WLT: A Radio Romance *(1992),* The Book of Guys *(1993),* Wobegon Boy *(1998), and* Me: By Jimmy (Big Boy) Valente *(1999).*

How to Write a Letter

BEFORE YOU READ: *In this age of cell phones and e-mail, the personal letter has almost become a thing of the past. Consider, however, what a letter can do that a phone call or electronic message cannot.*

TIPS FOR READING: *Keillor does not provide a numbered list of the steps in the process of writing a letter. Follow him as he first explains the need for writing letters and then goes into the process itself, letting breaks between paragraphs signal a move from one idea to the next.*

Words to Know:
wahoo	**an ignorant person**
sensuous	**appealing to the senses**
lit'ry	**short for** *literary,* **or having to do with literature**

TIPS FOR WRITING: *You may want a method more subtle than a numbered list to explain a process. Keillor explains the process of writing a letter from start to finish without resorting to such a numbered list.*

1   We shy persons need to write a letter now and then, or else we'll dry up and blow away. It's true. And I speak as one who loves to reach for the phone, dial the number, and talk. I say, "Big Bopper here—what's shakin', babes?" The telephone is to shyness what Hawaii is to February, it's a way out of the woods, *and yet:* a letter is better.

2   Such a sweet gift—a piece of handmade writing, in an envelope that is not a bill, sitting in our friend's path when she trudges home from a long

day spent among wahoos and savages, a day our words will help repair. They don't need to be immortal, just sincere. She can read them twice and again tomorrow: *You're someone I care about, Corinne, and think of often and every time I do you make me smile.*

3 We need to write, otherwise nobody will know who we are. They will have only a vague impression of us as A Nice Person, because, frankly; we don't shine at conversation, we lack the confidence to thrust our faces forward and say, "Hi, I'm Heather Hooten; let me tell you about my week." Mostly we say "Uh-huh" and "Oh, really." People smile and look over our shoulder, looking for someone else to meet.

4 So a shy person sits down and writes a letter. To be known by another person—to meet and talk freely on the page—to be close despite distance. To escape from anonymity and be our own sweet selves and express the music of our souls.

5 Same thing that moves a giant rock star to sing his heart out in front of 123,000 people moves us to take ballpoint in hand and write a few lines to our dear Aunt Eleanor. *We want to be known.* We want her to know that we have fallen in love, that we quit our job, that we're moving to New York, and we want to say a few things that might not get said in casual conversation: *Thank you for what you've meant to me, I am very happy right now.*

6 The first step in writing letters is to get over the guilt of *not* writing. You don't "owe" anybody a letter. Letters are a gift. The burning shame you feel when you see unanswered mail makes it harder to pick up a pen and makes for a cheerless letter when you finally do. *I feel bad about not writing, but I've been so busy,* etc. Skip this. Few letters are obligatory, and they are *Thanks for the wonderful gift* and *I am terribly sorry to hear about George's death* and *Yes, you're welcome to stay with us next month,* and not many more than that. Write those promptly if you want to keep your friends. Don't worry about the others, except love letters, of course. When your true love writes, *Dear Light of My Life, Joy of My Heart, O Lovely Pulsating Core of My Sensate Life,* some response is called for.

7 Some of the best letters are tossed off in a burst of inspiration, so keep your writing stuff in one place where you can sit down for a few minutes and (*Dear Roy, I am in the middle of a book entitled* We Are Still Married *but thought I'd drop you a line. Hi to your sweetie, too*) dash off a note to a pal. Envelopes, stamps, address book, everything in a drawer so you can write fast when the pen is hot.

8 A blank white eight-by-eleven sheet can look as big as Montana if the pen's not so hot—try a smaller page and write boldly. Or use a note card with a piece of fine art on the front; if your letter ain't good, at least they get

the Matisse. Get a pen that makes a sensuous line, get a comfortable type-writer, a friendly word processor—whichever feels easy to the hand.

9   Sit for a few minutes with the blank sheet in front of you, and meditate on the person you will write to, let your friend come to mind until you can almost see her or him in the room with you. Remember the last time you saw each other and how your friend looked and what you said and what perhaps was un-said between you, and when your friend becomes real to you, start to write.

10   Write the salutation—*Dear* You—and take a deep breath and plunge in. A simple declarative sentence will do, followed by another and another and another. Tell us what you're doing and tell it like you were talking to us. Don't think about grammar, don't think about lit'ry style, don't try to write dramatically, just give us your news. Where did you go, who did you see, what did they say, what do you think?

11   If you don't know where to begin, start with the present moment: *I'm sitting at the kitchen table on a rainy Saturday morning. Everyone is gone and the house is quiet.* Let your simple description of the present moment lead to something else, let the letter drift gently along.

12   The toughest letter to crank out is one that is meant to impress, as we all know from writing job applications; if it's hard work to slip off a letter to a friend, maybe you're trying too hard to be terrific. A letter is only a report to someone who already likes you for reasons other than your brilliance. Take it easy.

13   Don't worry about form. It's not a term paper. When you come to the end of one episode, just start a new paragraph. You can go from a few lines about the sad state of pro football to the fight with your mother to your fond memories of Mexico to your cat's urinary-tract infection to a few thoughts on personal indebtedness and on to the kitchen sink and what's in it. The more you write, the easier it gets, and when you have a True True Friend to write to, a *compadre,* a soul sibling, then it's like driving a car down a coun-try road, you just get behind the keyboard and press on the gas.

14   Don't tear up the page and start over when you write a bad line—try to write your way out of it. Make mistakes and plunge on. Let the letter cook along and let yourself be bold. Outrage, confusion, love—whatever is in your mind, let it find a way to the page. Writing is a means of discovery, al-ways, and when you come to the end and write *Yours ever* or *Hugs and kisses,* you'll know something you didn't when you wrote *Dear Pal.*

15   Probably your friend will put your letter away, and it'll be read again a few years from now—and it will improve with age. And forty years from now, your friend's grandkids will dig it out of the attic and read it, a sweet and precious relic of the ancient eighties that gives them a sudden clear

glimpse of you and her and the world we old-timers knew. You will then have created an object of art. Your simple lines about where you went, who you saw, what they said, will speak to those children and they will feel in their hearts the humanity of our times.

16   You can't pick up a phone and call the future and tell them about our times. You have to pick up a piece of paper.

Understanding Meaning

1. What does Keillor say in the first four paragraphs about why shy people need to write letters? Why is a letter better than a phone call?
2. What positive things can a letter do for the person who receives it?
3. What situations does Keillor say require writing a letter?
4. What advice does Keillor give his readers to help them get past any discomfort they might feel about starting a letter?
5. What, according to Keillor, should the writer of a letter not do?
6. At the end, why does he say the letter may have a lasting significance?
7. *CRITICAL THINKING.* In this age of e-mail and cell phones, is Keillor's advice outdated? Why or why not?

Evaluating Strategy

1. Why is it ironic that this particular author presents himself as a shy person?
2. How does Keillor make writing a letter sound easy while at the same time making clear how much a letter can mean to the person it is written to?
3. Keillor does not provide a numbered list of steps. Is the process of writing a letter made clear anyway? Explain.
4. Why does Keillor make use of italics?

Appreciating Language

1. Does Keillor sometimes break rules that English teachers try to teach us, like always writing in complete sentences? What effect does that have on the essay?
2. How does Keillor's word choice make readers feel that he is speaking very directly to them, in an informal manner?
3. Does Keillor's language sometimes seem exaggerated? Where? Does that weaken the effect of the essay?

Writing Suggestions

1. Write a paragraph in which you describe your experience as a letter writer. Was there a point at which e-mail took over, and you stopped writing letters?
2. *COLLABORATIVE WRITING.* Keillor says that we write to be known. Today we tend to know some of our correspondents primarily through their electronic messages. Work with your group to make a list of clues that you get from e-mail about the type of person who is writing.
3. Use what you learned in Writing Suggestion #2 above to write one to two paragraphs in which you explain how writers are "known" through clues they provide in their e-mails.

Excerpt from the

NARRATIVE OF THE LIFE OF

FREDERICK DOUGLASS

AN AMERICAN SLAVE.

WRITTEN BY HIMSELF.

BOSTON

**PUBLISHED AT THE ANTI-SLAVERY OFFICE,
NO. 25 CORNHILL
1845**

Title: The Narrative of the Life of Frederick Douglass
       An American Slave

Author: Frederick Douglass

Release Date: January 10, 2006 [EBook #23]

Language: English

Character set encoding: ASCII

    Note from the original file: This electronic book is being released
at this time to honor the birthday of Martin Luther King Jr. [Born
January 15, 1929] [Officially celebrated January 20, 1992]

Excerpt from CHAPTER VI

Very soon after I went to live with Mr. and Mrs. Auld, she very kindly commenced to teach me the A, B, C. After I had learned this, she assisted me in learning to spell words of three or four letters. Just at this point of my progress, Mr. Auld found out what was going on, and at once forbade Mrs. Auld to instruct me further, telling her, among other things, that it was unlawful, as well as unsafe, to teach a slave to read. To use his own words, further, he said, "If you give a nigger an inch, he will take an ell. A nigger should know nothing but to obey his master—to do as he is told to do. Learning would *spoil* the best nigger in the world. Now," said he, "if you teach that nigger (speaking of myself) how to read, there would be no keeping him. It would forever unfit him to be a slave. He would at once become unmanageable, and of no value to his master. As to himself, it could do him no good, but a great deal of harm. It would make him discontented and unhappy." These words sank deep into my heart, stirred up sentiments within that lay slumbering, and called into existence an entirely new train of thought. It was a new and special revelation, explaining dark and mysterious things, with which my youthful understanding had struggled, but struggled in vain. I now understood what had been to me a most perplexing difficulty—to wit, the white man's power to enslave the black man. It was a grand achievement, and I prized it highly. From that moment, I understood the pathway from slavery to freedom. It was just what I wanted, and I got it at a time when I the least expected it. Whilst I was saddened by the thought of losing the aid of my kind mistress, I was gladdened by the invaluable instruction which, by the merest accident, I had gained from my master. Though conscious of the difficulty of learning without a teacher, I set out with high hope, and a fixed purpose, at whatever cost of trouble, to learn how to read. The very decided manner with which he spoke, and strove to impress his wife with the evil consequences of giving me instruction, served to convince me that he was deeply sensible of the truths he was uttering. It gave me the best assurance that I might rely with the utmost confidence on the results which, he said, would flow from teaching me to read. What he most dreaded, that I most desired. What he most loved, that I most hated. That which to him was a great evil, to be carefully shunned, was to me a great good, to be diligently sought; and the argument which he so warmly urged, against my learning to read, only served to inspire me with a desire and determination to learn. In learning to read, I owe almost as much to the bitter opposition of my master, as to the kindly aid of my mistress. I acknowledge the benefit of both.

I had resided but a short time in Baltimore before I observed a marked difference, in the treatment of slaves, from that which I had witnessed in the country. A city slave is almost a freeman, compared with a slave on the plantation. He is much better fed and clothed, and enjoys privileges altogether unknown to the slave on the plantation. There is a vestige of decency, a sense of shame, that does much to curb and check those outbreaks of atrocious cruelty so commonly enacted upon the plantation. He is a desperate slaveholder, who will shock the humanity of his non-slaveholding neighbors with the cries of his lacerated slave. Few are willing to incur the odium attaching to the reputation of being a cruel master; and above all things, they would not be known as not giving a slave enough to eat. Every city slaveholder is anxious to have it known of him, that he feeds his slaves well; and it is due to them to say, that most of them do give their slaves enough to eat. There are, however, some painful exceptions to this rule. Directly opposite to us, on Philpot Street, lived Mr. Thomas Hamilton. He owned two slaves. Their names were Henrietta and Mary. Henrietta was about twenty-two years of age, Mary was about fourteen; and of all the mangled and emaciated creatures I ever looked upon, these two were the most so. His heart must be harder than stone, that could look upon these unmoved. The head, neck, and shoulders of Mary were literally cut to pieces. I have frequently felt her head, and found it nearly covered with festering sores, caused by the lash of her cruel mistress. I do not know that her master ever whipped her, but I have been an eye-witness to the cruelty of Mrs. Hamilton. I used to be in Mr. Hamilton's house nearly every day. Mrs. Hamilton used to sit in a large chair in the middle of the room, with a heavy cowskin always by her side, and scarce an hour passed during the day but was marked by the blood of one of these slaves. The girls seldom passed her without her saying, "Move faster, you *black gip!*" at the same time giving them a blow with the cowskin over the head or shoulders, often drawing the blood. She would then say, "Take that, you *black gip!*" continuing, "If you don't move faster, I'll move you!" Added to the cruel lashings to which these slaves were subjected, they were kept nearly half-starved.

They seldom knew what it was to eat a full meal. I have seen Mary contending with the pigs for the offal thrown into the street. So much was Mary kicked and cut to pieces, that she was oftener called "*pecked*" than by her name.

CHAPTER VII

I lived in Master Hugh's family about seven years. During this time, I succeeded in learning to read and write. In accomplishing this, I was compelled to resort to various stratagems. I had no regular teacher. My mistress, who had kindly commenced to instruct me, had, in compliance with the advice and direction of her husband, not only ceased to instruct, but had set her face against my being instructed by any one else. It is due, however, to my mistress to say of her, that she did not adopt this course of treatment immediately. She at first lacked the depravity indispensable to shutting me up in mental darkness. It was at least necessary for her to have some training in the exercise of irresponsible power, to make her equal to the task of treating me as though I were a brute.

My mistress was, as I have said, a kind and tenderhearted woman; and in the simplicity of her soul she commenced, when I first went to live with her, to treat me as she supposed one human being ought to treat another. In entering upon the duties of a slaveholder, she did not seem to perceive that I sustained to her the relation of a mere chattel, and that for her to treat me as a human being was not only wrong, but dangerously so. Slavery proved as injurious to her as it did to me. When I went there, she was a pious, warm, and tender-hearted woman. There was no sorrow or suffering for which she had not a tear. She had bread for the hungry, clothes for the naked, and comfort for every mourner that came within her reach. Slavery soon proved its ability to divest her of these heavenly qualities. Under its influence, the tender heart became stone, and the lamblike disposition gave way to one of tiger-like fierceness. The first step in her downward course was in her ceasing to instruct me. She now commenced to practise her husband's precepts. She finally became even more violent in her opposition than her husband himself. She was not satisfied with simply doing as well as he had commanded; she seemed anxious to do better. Nothing seemed to make her more angry than to see me with a newspaper. She seemed to think that here lay the danger. I have had her rush at me with a face made all up of fury, and snatch from me a newspaper, in a manner that fully revealed her apprehension. She was an apt woman; and a little experience soon demonstrated, to her satisfaction, that education and slavery were incompatible with each other.

From this time I was most narrowly watched. If I was in a separate room any considerable length of time, I was sure to be suspected of having a book, and was at once called to give an account of myself. All this, however, was too late. The first step had been taken. Mistress, in teaching me the alphabet, had given me the *inch,* and no precaution could prevent me from taking the *ell.*

The plan which I adopted, and the one by which I was most successful, was that of making friends of all the little white boys whom I met in the street. As many of these as I could, I converted into teachers. With their kindly aid, obtained at different times and in different places, I finally succeeded in learning to read. When I was sent of errands, I always took my book with me, and by going one part of my errand quickly, I found time to get a lesson before my return. I used also to carry bread with me, enough of which was always in the house, and to which I was always welcome; for I was much better off in this regard than many of the poor white children in our neighborhood. This bread I used to bestow upon the hungry little urchins, who, in return, would give me that more valuable bread of knowledge. I am strongly tempted to give the names of two or three of those little boys, as a testimonial of the gratitude and affection I bear them; but prudence forbids;—not that it would injure me, but it might embarrass them; for it is almost an unpardonable offence to teach slaves to read in this Christian country. It is enough to say of the dear little fellows, that they lived on Philpot Street, very near Durgin and Bailey's ship-yard. I used to talk this matter of slavery over with them. I would sometimes say to them, I wished I could be as free as they would be when they got to be men. "You will be free as soon as you are twenty-one, *but I am a slave for life!* Have not I as good a right to be free as you have?" These words used to trouble them; they would express for me the liveliest sympathy, and console me with the hope that something would occur by which I might be free.

I was now about twelve years old, and the thought of being *a slave for life* began to bear heavily upon my heart. Just about this time, I got hold of a book entitled "The Columbian Orator." Every opportunity I got, I used to read this book. Among much of other interesting matter, I found in it a dialogue between a master and his slave. The slave was represented as having run away from his master three times. The dialogue represented the conversation which took place between them, when the slave was retaken the third time. In this dialogue, the whole argument in behalf of slavery was brought forward by the master, all of which was disposed of by the slave. The slave was made to say some very smart as well as impressive things in reply to his master—things which had the desired though unexpected effect; for the conversation resulted in the voluntary emancipation of the slave on the part of the master.

In the same book, I met with one of Sheridan's mighty speeches on and in behalf of Catholic emancipation. These were choice documents to me. I read them over and over again with unabated interest. They gave tongue to interesting thoughts of my own soul, which had frequently flashed through my mind, and died away for want of utterance. The moral which I gained from the dialogue was the power of truth over the conscience of even a slaveholder. What I got from Sheridan was a bold denunciation of slavery, and a powerful vindication of human rights. The reading of these documents enabled me to utter my thoughts, and to meet the arguments brought forward to sustain slavery; but while they relieved me of one difficulty, they brought on another even more painful than the one of which I was relieved. The more I read, the more I was led to abhor and detest my enslavers. I could regard them in no other light than a band of successful robbers, who had left their homes, and gone to Africa, and stolen us from our homes, and in a strange land reduced us to slavery. I loathed them as being the meanest as well as the most wicked of men. As I read and contemplated the subject, behold! that very discontentment which Master Hugh had predicted would follow my learning to read had already come, to torment and sting my soul to unutterable anguish. As I writhed under it, I would at times feel that learning to read had been a curse rather than a blessing. It had given me a view of my wretched condition, without the remedy. It opened my eyes to the horrible pit, but to no ladder upon which to get out. In moments of agony, I envied my fellow-slaves for their stupidity. I have often wished myself a beast. I preferred the condition of the meanest reptile to my own. Any thing, no matter what, to get rid of thinking! It was this everlasting thinking of my condition that tormented me. There was no getting rid of it. It was pressed upon me by every object within sight or hearing, animate or inanimate. The silver trump of freedom had roused my soul to eternal wakefulness. Freedom now appeared, to disappear no more forever. It was heard in every sound, and seen in every thing. It was ever present to torment me with a sense of my wretched condition. I saw nothing without seeing it, I heard nothing without hearing it, and felt nothing without feeling it. It looked from every star, it smiled in every calm, breathed in every wind, and moved in every storm.

I often found myself regretting my own existence, and wishing myself dead; and but for the hope of being free, I have no doubt but that I should have killed myself, or done something for which I should have been killed. While in this state of mind, I was eager to hear any one speak of slavery. I was a ready listener. Every little while, I could hear something about the abolitionists. It was some time before I found what the word meant. It was always used in such connections as to make it an interesting word to me. If a slave ran away and succeeded in getting clear, or if a slave killed his master, set fire to a barn, or did any thing very wrong in the mind of a slaveholder, it was spoken of as the fruit of *abolition.* Hearing the word in this connection very often, I set about learning what it meant. The dictionary afforded me little or no help. I found it was "the act of abolishing;" but then I did not know what was to be abolished. Here I was perplexed. I did not dare to ask any one about its meaning, for I was satisfied that it was something they wanted me to know very little about. After a patient waiting, I got one of our city papers, containing an account of the number of petitions from the north, praying for the abolition of slavery in the District of Columbia, and of the slave trade between the States. From this time I understood the words *abolition* and *abolitionist,* and always drew near when that word was spoken, expecting to hear something of importance to myself and fellow-slaves. The light broke in upon me by degrees. I went one day down on the wharf of Mr. Waters; and seeing two Irishmen unloading a scow of stone, I went, unasked, and helped them. When we had finished, one of them came to me and asked me if I were a slave. I told him I was.

He asked, "Are ye a slave for life?" I told him that I was. The good Irishman seemed to be deeply affected by the statement. He said to the other that it was a pity so fine a little fellow as myself should be a slave for life. He said it was a shame to hold me. They both advised me to run away to the north; that I should find friends there, and that I should be free. I pretended not to be interested in what they said, and treated them as if I did not understand them; for I feared they might be treacherous. White men have been known to encourage slaves to escape, and then, to get the reward, catch them and return them to their masters. I was afraid that these seemingly good men might use me so; but I nevertheless remembered their advice, and from that time I resolved to run away. I looked forward to a time at which it would be safe for me to escape. I was too young to think of doing so immediately; besides, I wished to learn how to write, as I might have occasion to write my own pass. I consoled myself with the hope that I should one day find a good chance. Meanwhile, I would learn to write.

The idea as to how I might learn to write was suggested to me by being in Durgin and Bailey's ship-yard, and frequently seeing the ship carpenters, after hewing, and getting a piece of timber ready for use, write on the timber the name of that part of the ship for which it was intended. When a piece of timber was intended for the larboard side, it would be marked thus—"L." When a piece was for the starboard side, it would be marked thus—"S." A piece for the larboard side forward, would be marked thus—"L. F." When a piece was for starboard side forward, it would be marked thus—"S. F." For larboard aft, it would be marked thus—"L. A." For starboard aft, it would be marked thus—"S. A." I soon learned the names of these letters, and for what they were intended when placed upon a piece of timber in the ship-yard. I immediately commenced copying them, and in a short time was able to make the four letters named. After that, when I met with any boy who I knew could write, I would tell him I could write as well as he. The next word would be, "I don't believe you. Let me see you try it." I would then make the letters which I had been so fortunate as to learn, and ask him to beat that. In this way I got a good many lessons in writing, which it is quite possible I should never have gotten in any other way. During this time, my copy-book was the board fence, brick wall, and pavement; my pen and ink was a lump of chalk. With these, I learned mainly how to write. I then commenced and continued copying the Italics in Webster's Spelling Book, until I could make them all without looking on the book. By this time, my little Master Thomas had gone to school, and learned how to write, and had written over a number of copy-books. These had been brought home, and shown to some of our near neighbors, and then laid aside. My mistress used to go to class meeting at the Wilk Street meetinghouse every Monday afternoon, and leave me to take care of the house. When left thus, I used to spend the time in writing in the spaces left in Master Thomas's copy-book, copying what he had written. I continued to do this until I could write a hand very similar to that of Master Thomas. Thus, after a long, tedious effort for years, I finally succeeded in learning how to write.

5

MALCOLM X

Malcolm X (1925–1965) was born Malcolm Little in Omaha, Nebraska. While serving a prison sentence for burglary (1946–52), he converted to the Nation of Islam, a black separatist group founded by Elijah Muhammad. After being paroled, Little changed his name to Malcolm X and became the most visible spokesman for the Nation of Islam (popularly known as Black Muslims). By the 1960s, he broke with Elijah Muhammad, converted to orthodox Islam, and changed his name to el-Hajj Malik el-Shabazz. A pilgrimage to the holy city of Mecca caused him to abandon racial separatism and embrace the ideal of human brotherhood. Malcolm X was assassinated while speaking at a Harlem rally in 1965.

Prison Studies

BEFORE YOU READ: *Malcolm X explains how it was only in prison that he found the freedom to educate himself.*

TIPS FOR READING: *As you read, mark the two or three sentences that you feel most directly sum up the author's main idea in this passage.*

Words to Know:

emulate	to try to equal or surpass
riffling	to leaf rapidly through
engrossing	taking one's entire attention, absorbing
feign	pretend
dormant	as if asleep, inactive

1   Many who today hear me somewhere in person, or on television, or those who read something I've said, will think I went to school far beyond the eighth grade. This impression is due entirely to my prison studies.

2   It had really begun back in the Charlestown Prison, when Bimbi first made me feel envy of his stock of knowledge. Bimbi had always taken charge of any conversation he was in, and I had tried to emulate him. But every book I picked up had few sentences which didn't contain anywhere from one to nearly all of the words that might as well have been in Chinese. When I just skipped those words, of course, I really ended up with little idea of what the book said. So I had come to the Norfolk

Prison Colony still going through only book-reading motions. Pretty soon, I would have quit even these motions, unless I had received the motivation that I did.

3   I saw that the best thing I could do was get hold of a dictionary—to study, to learn some words. I was lucky enough to reason also that I should try to improve my penmanship. It was sad. I couldn't even write in a straight line. It was both ideas together that moved me to request a dictionary along with some tablets and pencils from the Norfolk Prison Colony school.

4   I spent two days just riffling uncertainly through the dictionary's pages. I'd never realized so many words existed! I didn't know which words I needed to learn. Finally, to start some kind of action, I began copying.

5   In my slow, painstaking, ragged handwriting, I copied into my tablet everything printed on that first page, down to the punctuation marks.

6   I believe it took me a day. Then, aloud, I read back, to myself, everything I'd written on the tablet. Over and over, aloud to myself, I read my own handwriting.

7   I woke up the next morning, thinking about those words—immensely proud to realize that not only had I written so much at one time, but I'd written words that I never knew were in the world. Moreover, with a little effort, I also could remember what many of these words meant. I reviewed the words whose meanings I didn't remember. Funny thing, from the dictionary first page right now, that "aardvark" springs to my mind. The dictionary had a picture of it, a long-tailed, long-eared, burrowing African mammal, which lives off termites caught by sticking out its tongue as an anteater does for ants.

8   I was so fascinated that I went on—I copied the dictionary's next page. And the same experience came when I studied that. With every succeeding page, I also learned of people and places and events from history. Actually the dictionary is like a miniature encyclopedia. Finally the dictionary's A section had filled a whole tablet—and I went on into the B's. That was the way I started copying what eventually became the entire dictionary. It went a lot faster after so much practice helped me to pick up handwriting speed. Between what I wrote in my tablet, and writing letters, during the rest of my time in prison I would guess I wrote a million words.

9   I suppose it was inevitable that as my word-base broadened, I could for the first time pick up a book and read and now begin to understand what the book was saying. Anyone who has read a great deal can imagine the new world that opened. Let me tell you something: from then until I left the prison, in every free moment I had, if I was not reading in the library, I was reading on my bunk. You couldn't have gotten me out of books with a wedge. Between Mr. Muhammad's teachings, my correspondence, my visitors—usually Ella and Reginald—and my reading of books, months

passed without my even thinking about being imprisoned. In fact, up to then, I never had been so truly free in my life.

10   As you can imagine, especially in a prison where there was heavy emphasis on rehabilitation, an inmate was smiled upon if he demonstrated an unusually intense interest in books. There was a sizable number of well-read inmates, especially the popular debaters. Some were said by many to be practically walking encyclopedias. They were almost celebrities. No university would ask any student to devour literature as I did when this new world opened to me, of being able to read and *understand*.

11   I read more in my room than in the library itself. An inmate who was known to read a lot could check out more than the permitted maximum number of books. I preferred reading in the total isolation of my own room.

12   When I had progressed to really serious reading, every night at about ten p.m. I would be outraged with the "lights out." It always seemed to catch me right in the middle of something engrossing.

13   Fortunately, right outside my door was a corridor light that cast a glow into my room. The glow was enough to read by, once my eyes adjusted to it. So when "lights out" came, I would sit on the floor where I could continue reading in that glow.

14   At one-hour intervals the night guards paced past every room. Each time I heard the approaching footsteps, I jumped into bed and feigned sleep. And as soon as the guard passed, I got back out of bed onto the floor area of that light-glow, where I would read for another fifty-eight minutes—until the guard approached again. That went on until three or four every morning. Three or four hours of sleep a night was enough for me. Often in the years in the streets I had slept less than that.

15   I have often reflected upon the new vistas that reading opened to me. I knew right there in prison that reading had changed forever the course of my life. As I see it today, the ability to read awoke inside me some long dormant craving to be mentally alive. I certainly wasn't seeking any degree, the way a college confers a status symbol upon its students. My homemade education gave me, with every additional book that I read, a little bit more sensitivity to the deafness, dumbness, and blindness that was afflicting the black race in America. Not long ago, an English writer telephoned me from London asking questions. One was "What's your alma mater?" I told him, "Books." You will never catch me with a free fifteen minutes in which I'm not studying something I feel might be able to help the black man.

16   Every time I catch a plane, I have with me a book that I want to read—and that's a lot of books these days. If I weren't out here every day battling the white man, I could spend the rest of my life reading, just sat-

isfying my curiosity—because you can hardly mention anything I'm not curious about. I don't think anybody ever got more out of going to prison than I did. In fact, prison enabled me to study far more intensively than I would have if my life had gone differently and I had attended some college. I imagine that one of the biggest troubles with colleges is there are too many distractions, too much panty-raiding, fraternities, and boola-boola and all of that. Where else but in prison could I have attacked my ignorance by being able to study intensely sometimes as much as fifteen hours a day?

Understanding Meaning

1. Malcolm X tells us that he had only an eighth-grade education and that before he started his "homemade education" in prison, he went through only "book-reading motions." What made him decide that this limited education was not enough?
2. What method did Malcolm X use to increase his vocabulary and improve his handwriting?
3. How could Malcolm X, while still in prison, honestly say, "I never had been so truly free in my life"?

Evaluating Strategy

1. *BLENDING THE MODES.* The first three paragraphs of the piece do not explain *how* Malcolm X learned to read and write well. Rather, they establish *why* he wanted to. The second-to-last paragraph explains how he was affected by his studies. Did this structure make the organization easy to follow? Why or why not?

Appreciating Language

1. How would you characterize Malcolm X's language? Is his diction lofty or commonplace? Is the passage easy or difficult to read? Why?
2. At other times, Malcolm X used such emotional language as referring to a white person as a "devil" and to "how the white man's society was responsible for the black man's condition in this wilderness of North America." Overall, does the tone of this essay seem to be emotional and angry, or is there a different sort of tone? If not an angry voice, what sort of voice do you hear speaking in the excerpt?

Writing Suggestions

1. Write a paragraph in which you tell about a time when something you read had an emotional impact on you. It should be clear to your readers what emotion it aroused in you.

2. *PREWRITING.* Take about five minutes to jot down a list of the different types of things you write. They could be anything from grocery lists to term papers. Include writing that you do in electronic form. Try to list at least 10–12 types of writing. Then start grouping together the ones that seem to go together. What categories do they fall into?

3. Use the clusters you created in Writing Suggestion #2 above to structure an essay explaining the functions that writing serves in your life. What sort of a thesis will you need? What might the conclusion look like? Consider, for example, types of writing that you never find time for and others that you must find time for.

6

NAT HENTOFF

Nat Hentoff (1925–) was born in Boston. The author of more than 25 books, Hentoff is also known for his numerous articles in the Village Voice, New Yorker, *and the* Washington Post. *A committed liberal, he has been outspoken on issues ranging from drug testing and the draft to racism and abortion. Although considered a leftist, Hentoff has criticized those on the Left who have advocated suppressing what they consider "hate speech."*

Should This Student Have Been Expelled?

BEFORE YOU READ: *You have probably heard the comment that the right to free speech does not give you the right to cry "Fire!" in a crowded theater. When is speech unacceptable? Some colleges have passed "hate speech" codes that prohibit racist and sexist "actions." In this article Hentoff asks whether a college student should have been expelled for making offensive statements.*

TIPS FOR READING: *Hentoff begins the essay by relating the events of October 18, 1990, and then explains Brown University's response. Notice how Hentoff builds his argument by quoting and analyzing the university speech code and President Gregorian's statements. Consider your own definitions of "speech" and "action." When does speech become action?*

> **Words to Know:**
>
> | | |
> |---|---|
> | imbibed | consumed, drunk |
> | juncture | point in time |
> | penance | apology, atonement |
> | enshrined | made permanent |
> | detached | objective |
> | dissenters | those who protest or object |
> | flagrant | very obvious |
> | tenor | mood |

The day that Brown denies any student freedom of speech is the day I give up my presidency of the university.
—Vartan Gregorian, president of Brown University,
February 20, 1991

"Should This Student Have Been Expelled?" by Nat Hentoff from VILLAGE VOICE, 1991. Reprinted by permission of Nat Hentoff, columnist, Village Voice.

1   Doug Hann, a varsity football player at Brown, was also concentrating on organizational behavior and management and business economics. On the night of October 18, 1990, Hann, a junior, was celebrating his twenty-first birthday, and in the process had imbibed a considerable amount of spirits.

2   At one point, Hann shouted into the air, "Fuck you, niggers!" It was aimed at no one in particular but apparently at all black students at Brown. Or in the world. A freshman leaned out a dormitory window and asked him to stop being so loud and offensive.

3   Hann, according to reporters on the *Brown Daily Herald*, looked up and yelled, "What are you, a faggot?" Hann then noticed an Israeli flag in the dorm. "What are you, a Jew?" he shouted. "Fucking Jew!"

4   Hann had achieved the hat trick of bigotry. (In hockey, the hat trick is scoring three goals in a game.) In less than a minute, Hann had engaged in racist, anti-Semitic, and homophobic insults.

5   He wasn't through. As reported by Smita Nerula in the *Brown Daily Herald*, the freshman who had asked Hann to cool it recruited a few people from his dorm "and followed Hann and his friends."

6   "This resulted in a verbal confrontation outside of Wayland Arch. At this time, [Hann] was said to have turned to one of the freshman's friends, a black woman, and shouted, 'My parents own your people.'"

7   To the Jewish student, or the student he thought was Jewish, Hann said, "Happy Hanukkah."

8   There are reports that at this juncture Hann tried to fight some of the students who had been following him. But, the *Brown Daily Herald* reports, he "was held back by one of his friends, while [another] friend stretched his arm across the Wayland Gates to keep the students from following Hann."

9   John Howard Crouch—a student and Brown chapter secretary of the American Civil Liberties Union there—tells me that because Hann had friends restraining him, "nobody seriously expected fighting, regardless of anyone's words."

10 Anyway, there was no physical combat. Just words. Awful words, but nothing more than speech. (Nor were there any threats.)

11 This was not the first time Hann's graceful drunken language had surfaced at Brown. Two years before, in an argument with a black student at a fraternity bar, Hann had called the student a "nigger." Thereupon he had been ordered to attend a race relations workshop and to get counseling for possible alcohol abuse. Obviously, he has not been rehabilitated.

12 Months went by after Hann's notorious birthday celebration as Brown's internal disciplinary procedures cranked away. (To steal a phrase from

Robert Sherrill, Brown's way of reaching decisions in these matters is to due process as military music is to music. But that's true of any college or university I know anything about.)

13   At last, the Undergraduate Disciplinary Council (five faculty or administration members and five students) ruled that Doug Hann was to leave the university forevermore. Until two years ago, it was possible for a Brown student to be dismissed, which meant that he or she could reapply after a decent period of penance. But now, Brown has enshrined the sentence of expulsion. You may go on to assist Mother Teresa in caring for the dying or you may teach a course in feminism to 2 Live Crew, but no accomplishments, no matter how noble, will get you back into Brown once you have been expelled.

14   Doug Hann will wander the earth without a Brown degree for the rest of his days.

15   The president of Brown, Vartan Gregorian—formerly the genial head of the New York Public Library—had the power to commute or even reverse the sentence. But the speech code under which Hann was thrown out had been proposed by Gregorian himself shortly after he was inaugurated in 1989, so he was hardly a detached magistrate.

16   On January 25, 1991, Vartan Gregorian affirmed, with vigor, the expulsion decision by the Undergraduate Disciplinary Council.

17   Hann became a historic figure. Under all the "hate speech" codes enacted around the country in recent years, he is the first student to actually be expelled for violating one of the codes.

18   The *New York Times* (February 12) reported that "Howard Ehrlich, the research director of the National Institute Against Prejudice and Violence, said that he did not know of any other such expulsions, but that he was familiar with cases in which students who had harassed others were moved to other dormitories or ordered to undergo counseling."

19   But that takes place in *educational* institutions, whose presidents recognize that there are students who need help, not exile.

20   At first, there didn't seem to be much protest among the student body at Brown on free speech grounds—except for members of the Brown chapter of the ACLU and some free thinkers on the student paper, as well as some unaffiliated objectors to expelling students for what they say, not for what they do. The number of these dissenters is increasing, as we shall see.

21   At the student paper, however, the official tone has changed from the libertarian approach of Vernon Silver, who was editor-in-chief last semester. A February 13 *Brown Daily Herald* editorial was headed: *"Good Riddance."*

22   It began: "Doug Hann is gone, and the university is well to be rid of him."

23   But President Gregorian has been getting a certain amount of flack and so, smiting his critics hip and thigh, he wrote a letter to the *New York Times*. Well, that letter (printed on February 21) was actually a press release, distributed by the Brown University News Bureau to all sorts of people, including me, on February 12. There were a few changes—and that *Brown Daily Herald* editorial was attached to it—but Gregorian's declaration was clearly not written exclusively for the *Times*.

24   Is this a new policy at the *Times*—taking public relations handouts for the letters page?

25   Next week I shall include a relentlessly accurate analysis of President Gregorian's letter by the executive director of the Rhode Island ACLU. But first, an account of what Gregorian said in that letter to the *Times*.

26   President Gregorian indignantly denies that Brown has ever expelled "anyone for the exercise of free speech, nor will it ever do so." Cross his heart.

27   He then goes into self-celebration: "My commitment to free speech and condemnation of racism and homophobia are well known. . . .

28   "The university's code of conduct does not prohibit speech; it prohibits *actions*."

29   Now watch this pitiable curve ball:

30   "Offence III [of the Brown code]—which deals with harassment—prohibits inappropriate, abusive, threatening, or demeaning actions based on race, religion, gender, handicap, ethnicity, national origin, or sexual orientation."

31   In the original press release, Gregorian underlined the word *actions*. There, and in the letter to the *Times*—lest a dozing reader miss the point—Gregorian emphasizes that "The rules do not proscribe words, epithets, or slanders, they proscribe behavior." Behavior that "shows flagrant disrespect for the well-being of others or is unreasonably disruptive of the University community."

32   Consider the overbreadth and vagueness of these penalty-bearing provisions. What are the definitions of "harassment," "inappropriate," "demeaning," "flagrant," "disrespect," "well-being," "unreasonably"?

33   Furthermore, with regard to Brown's termination of Doug Hann with extreme prejudice, Gregorian is engaging in the crudest form of Orwellian newspeak. Hann was kicked out for *speech*, and only speech—not for *actions*, as Gregorian huffily insists. As for behavior, the prickly folks whose burning of the American flag was upheld by the Supreme Court were indeed engaged in behavior, but that behavior was based entirely on symbolic speech. So was Hann's. He didn't punch anybody or vandalize any property. He brayed.

34   Art Spitzer, legal director of the ACLU's National Capital Area affiliate, wrote a personal letter to Gregorian:

35   "There is a very simple test for determining whether a person is being punished for his actions or his speech. You just ask whether he would have received the same punishment if he had spoken different words while engaging in the same conduct.

36   "Thus, would your student have been expelled if he had gotten drunk and stood in the same courtyard at the same hour of the night, shouting at the same decibel level, 'Black is Beautiful!' 'Gay is Good!' or 'Go Brown! Beat Yale!' or even 'Nuke Baghdad! Kill Saddam!'?"

37   "I am confident," Spitzer said, that "he would not have been expelled for such 'actions.' If that is correct, it follows that *he was expelled for the unsavory content of his speech*, and not for his actions. I have no doubt that you can understand this distinction. (Emphasis added.)

38   "Now, you are certainly entitled to believe that it is appropriate to expel a student for the content of his speech when that content is sufficiently offensive to the 'university community.' . . .

39   "If that is your position, why can't you deliver it forthrightly? Then the university community can have an open debate about which opinions it finds offensive, and ban them. Perhaps this can be done once a year, so that the university's rules can keep pace with the tenor of the times—after all, it wouldn't do to have outmoded rules banning procommunist or blasphemous speech still on the books, now that it's 1991. Then students and teachers applying for admission or employment at Brown will know what they are getting into.

40   "Your recent statements, denying the obvious, are just hypocritical. . . ."

41   And what did the *New York Times*—in a stunningly fatuous February 21 editorial—say of Vartan Gregorian's sending Doug Hann into permanent exile? "A noble attempt both to govern and teach."

42   The *Times* editorials should really be signed, so that the rest of the editorial board isn't blamed for such embarrassments.

Understanding Meaning

1.   What events led to Hann's expulsion? Why does Hentoff call him "a historic figure"?
2.   Can one make both a "commitment to free speech" and a "condemnation of racism"?

3. What are "hate speech" codes? Does it strike you as odd that no one seemed offended by Hann's use of the infamous "f-word"? Is obscenity less disturbing than racial slurs?
4. Would comments about Irish drunks or Italian gangsters be considered "hate speech"?
5. *CRITICAL THINKING.* How do you separate "speech" from "action"? Does the concept of free speech, for instance, allow one to insult a person without facing the legal consequences that would arise from a physical assault?

Evaluating Strategy

1. Hentoff begins his article with a quote from the president of Brown University. How does this set up his argument?
2. Label where Hentoff uses logical, emotional, and ethical appeals.
3. Do you find Hentoff's inclusion of the press release effective?
4. *BLENDING THE MODES.* Where does Hentoff use narration, comparison, and definition?

Appreciating Language

1. Hentoff refers to Hann's activity as a "hat trick of bigotry"—scoring racist, anti-Semitic, and homophobic insults in one outburst. Does the use of this hockey term suggest mockery? Would "triple threat" have different connotations?
2. What tone does Hentoff create with comments about military music and statements such as "Doug Hann will wander the earth without a Brown degree for the rest of his days"? How seriously does he seem to take the issue of "hate speech" and those who condemn it?

Writing Suggestions

1. Assume you were a student at Brown University during the Hann controversy. Write a short statement to the editor of the college paper arguing whether or not Hann should be expelled. Support your argument with more than one persuasive appeal.
2. *COLLABORATIVE WRITING.* Discuss the concept of hate speech with a group of students. Ask group members to consider the fate of Doug Hann. Should he have been expelled? Is "hate speech" protected by the Bill of Rights? Record comments, and write a brief argument for or against disciplining students for expressing racist statements.

7

MARY SHERRY

Mary Sherry (1940–) writes from her experience as a parent, a writer, and a teacher. She writes articles and advertising copy, owns a small publishing firm in Minnesota, and for many years has taught remedial and creative writing to adults.

In Praise of the "F" Word

BEFORE YOU READ: *Have you ever considered the possibility that making an F could be a positive learning experience?*

TIPS FOR READING: *Even if at first glance you don't feel you want to listen to someone who says more students should fail, read this piece with an open mind and find out what students who were passed when they should have failed now say about being passed along.*

Words to Know:

semiliterate	**knowing how to read and write a little**
impediments	**obstacles**
trump card	**in playing cards, an advantage held until one needs it**

1   Tens of thousands of 18-year-olds will graduate this year and be handed meaningless diplomas. These diplomas won't look any different from those awarded their luckier classmates. Their validity will be questioned only when their employers discover that these graduates are semiliterate.

2   Eventually a fortunate few will find their way into educational repair shops—adult-literacy programs, such as the one where I teach basic grammar and writing. There, high-school graduates and high-school dropouts pursuing graduate-equivalency certificates will learn the skills they should have learned in school. They will also discover they have been cheated by our educational system.

3   As I teach, I learn a lot about our schools. Early in each session I ask my students to write about an unpleasant experience they had in school. No writers' block here! "I wish someone would have made me stop doing drugs and made me study." "I liked to party and no one seemed to care." "I was a good kid and didn't cause any trouble, so they just passed me along even though I didn't read well and couldn't write." And so on.

"In Praise of the 'F' Word" by Mary Sherry as appeared in NEWSWEEK, May 6, 1991. Reprinted by permission of Mary Sherry.

4   I am your basic do-gooder, and prior to teaching this class I blamed the poor academic skills our kids have today on drugs, divorce and other impediments to concentration necessary for doing well in school. But, as I rediscover each time I walk into the classroom, before a teacher can expect students to concentrate, he has to get their attention, no matter what distractions may be at hand. There are many ways to do this, and they have much to do with teaching style. However, if style alone won't do it, there is another way to show who holds the winning hand in the classroom. That is to reveal the trump card of failure.

5   I will never forget a teacher who played that card to get the attention of one of my children. Our youngest, a world-class charmer, did little to develop his intellectual talents but always got by. Until Mrs. Stifter.

6   Our son was a high-school senior when he had her for English. "He sits in the back of the room talking to his friends," she told me. "Why don't you move him to the front row?" I urged, believing the embarrassment would get him to settle down. Mrs. Stifter looked at me steely-eyed over her glasses. "I don't move seniors," she said. "I flunk them." I was flustered. Our son's academic life flashed before my eyes. No teacher had ever threatened him with that before. I regained my composure and managed to say that I thought she was right. By the time I got home I was feeling pretty good about this. It was a radical approach for these times, but, well, why not? "She's going to flunk you," I told my son. I did not discuss it any further. Suddenly English became a priority in his life. He finished out the semester with an A.

7   I know one example doesn't make a case, but at night I see a parade of students who are angry and resentful for having been passed along until they could no longer even pretend to keep up. Of average intelligence or better, they eventually quit school, concluding they were too dumb to finish. "I should have been held back" is a comment I hear frequently. Even sadder are those students who are high-school graduates who say to me after a few weeks of class, "I don't know how I ever got a high-school diploma."

8   Passing students who have not mastered the work cheats them and the employers who expect graduates to have basic skills. We excuse this dishonest behavior by saying kids can't learn if they come from terrible environments. No one seems to stop to think that—no matter what environments they come from—most kids don't put school first on their list unless they perceive something is at stake. They'd rather be sailing.

9   Many students I see at night could give expert testimony on unemployment, chemical dependency, abusive relationships. In spite of these difficulties, they have decided to make education a priority. They are motivated by

the desire for a better job or the need to hang on to the one they've got. They have a healthy fear of failure.

10   People of all ages can rise above their problems, but they need to have a reason to do so. Young people generally don't have the maturity to value education in the same way my adult students value it. But fear of failure, whether economic or academic, can motivate both.

11   Flunking as a regular policy has just as much merit today as it did two generations ago. We must review the threat of flunking and see it as it really is—a positive teaching tool. It is an expression of confidence by both teachers and parents that the students have the ability to learn the material presented to them. However, making it work again would take a dedicated, caring conspiracy between teachers and parents. It would mean facing the tough reality that passing kids who haven't learned the material—while it might save them grief for the short term—dooms them to long-term illiteracy. It would mean that teachers would have to follow through on their threats, and parents would have to stand behind them, knowing their children's best interests are indeed at stake. This means no more doing Scott's assignments for him because he might fail. No more passing Jodi because she's such a nice kid.

12   This is a policy that worked in the past and can work today. A wise teacher, with the support of his parents, gave our son the opportunity to succeed—or fail. It's time we return this choice to all students.

Understanding Meaning

1. Why do Sherry's students feel that they have been cheated by the educational system? What does she try to help them do?
2. When Sherry discusses the students that she works with in night school, what reasons does she say they have for not doing well in school? How do they feel about their education when they look back on it?
3. Why are the students that Sherry teaches motivated to learn what they failed to learn when they were younger?
4. What is Sherry's solution to the problem?
5. Why does Sherry call the threat of failure a positive teaching tool?
6. Why would it take a concerted effort of parents and teachers for her suggestion to work?
7. *CRITICAL THINKING.* Do you feel that the threat of failure would motivate students to do better in school? Is Sherry right in thinking that students do not perceive failure to be a real threat? Have things changed since Sherry published this essay in 1991?

Evaluating Strategy

1. When Sherry (or her editors) chose the title for this 1991 article, they were obviously trying to capture the attention of their readers. Do you think it was a successful strategy? Why or why not?
2. Why is the first sentence one that might attract the attention of her readers and make them want to read on?
3. *BLENDING THE MODES*. Where does Sherry make use of examples to make her point?
4. Why might it be a good tactic to end the piece by advocating that students should be given a choice?

Appreciating Language

1. What does Sherry mean when she refers to failure as the "trump card" of education? What is the large metaphor that she is using?
2. What does Sherry suggest through her choice of the term *educational repair shops* in the second paragraph?
3. Do you see any other places where Sherry gets across her own particular bias on the subject through the words that she chooses? Where?

Writing Suggestions

1. Have you ever felt that you were cheated by our educational system? Explain in one to two paragraphs.
2. Write a paragraph in which you explain whether or not you agree with Sherry that failing students more often would solve some of the problems with today's schools.
3. *COLLABORATIVE WRITING*. Discuss Sherry's views with a group of students. Do they see flunking as a "positive teaching tool"? Record student comments and develop a short statement. If students disagree, develop opposing statements.

8

NIKKI GIOVANNI

Born in Tennessee and educated at Nashville's predominantly black Fisk University, Nikki Giovanni (1943–) is one of the more important poets to emerge from the American civil rights movement of the 1960s. Her books include Black Feeling, Black Talk *(1968),* Black Judgement *(1969),* Re:Creation *(1970),* Gemini: An Extended Autobiographical Statement on My First Twenty-Five Years Being a Black Poet *(1971),* My house *(1972),* The Men and the Women *(1975),* Cotton Candy on a Rainy Day *(1978),* Sacred Cow . . . and Other Edibles *(1988), and* Racism 101 *(1994). She is currently a professor of English at Virginia Institute of Technology.*

Campus Racism 101

BEFORE YOU READ: *Giovanni's title suggests an introductory college course, but the advice she offers African American students is information they won't learn in class.*

TIPS FOR READING: *It becomes clear by the middle of Giovanni's essay that she is speaking directly to African American students entering college. Any other students reading her essay should also stop to think, however, how her advice applies to them.*

> **Words to Know:**
> demeaning   **degrading, lowering in status or character**
> intimidating   **making timid or afraid**

TIPS FOR READING: *Giovanni does not present a list of steps that must be performed in a particular order, but rather a list of suggested behaviors that will help a college student be successful. Her essay can provide a model of how to present your readers with advice on any of a number of topics. Note that she uses the paragraphs leading into the list to explain the need for such advice.*

1   There is a bumper sticker that reads: TOO BAD IGNORANCE ISN'T PAINFUL. I like that. But ignorance is. We just seldom attribute the pain to it or recognize it when we see it. Like the postcard on my corkboard. It shows a young man in a very hip jacket smoking a cigarette. In the background is a high school with the American flag waving. The caption says: "Too cool for school. Yet too stupid for the real world." Out of the mouth of the young man is a bubble enclosing the words "Maybe I'll start a band." There could be a postcard showing a jock in a uniform saying, "I don't need school. I'm

going to the NFL or NBA." Or one showing a young man or woman studying and a group of young people saying, "So you want to be white." Or
something equally demeaning. We need to quit it.

2   I am a professor of English at Virginia Tech. I've been here for four
years, though for only two years with academic rank. I am tenured, which
means I have a teaching position for life, a rarity on a predominantly white
campus. Whether from malice or ignorance, people who think I should be
at a predominantly Black institution will ask, "Why are you at Tech?" Because it's here. And so are Black students. But even if Black students
weren't here, it's painfully obvious that this nation and this world cannot
allow white students to go through higher education without interacting
with Blacks in authoritative positions. It is equally clear that predominantly
Black colleges cannot accommodate the numbers of Black students who
want and need an education.

3   Is it difficult to attend a predominantly white college? Compared with
what? Being passed over for promotion because you lack credentials? Being
turned down for jobs because you are not college-educated? Joining the
armed forces or going to jail because you cannot find an alternative to the
streets? Let's have a little perspective here. Where can you go and what can
you do that frees you from interacting with the white American mentality?
You're going to interact; the only question is, will you be in some control of
yourself and your actions, or will you be controlled by others? I'm going to
recommend self-control.

4   What's the difference between prison and college? They both prescribe
your behavior for a given period of time. They both allow you to read books
and develop your writing. They both give you time alone to think and time
with your peers to talk about issues. But four years of prison doesn't give
you a passport to greater opportunities. Most likely that time only gives you
greater knowledge of how to get back in. Four years of college gives you an
opportunity not only to lift yourself but to serve your people effectively.
What's the difference when you are called nigger in college from when you
are called nigger in prison? In college you can, though I admit with effort,
follow procedures to have those students who called you nigger kicked out
or suspended. You can bring issues to public attention without risking your
life. But mostly, college is and always has been the future. We, neither less
nor more than other people, need knowledge. There are discomforts attached to attending predominantly white colleges, though no more so than
living in a racist world. Here are some rules to follow that may help:

5   *Go to class.* No matter how you feel. No matter how you think the professor feels about you. It's important to have a consistent presence in the

classroom. If nothing else, the professor will know you care enough and are serious enough to be there.

6   *Meet your professors.* Extend your hand (give a firm handshake) and tell them your name. Ask them what you need to do to make an A. You may never make an A, but you have put them on notice that you are serious about getting good grades.

7   *Do assignments on time.* Typed or computer-generated. You have the syllabus. Follow it, and turn those papers in. If for some reason you can't complete an assignment on time, let your professor know before it is due and work out a new due date—then meet it.

8   *Go back to see your professor.* Tell him or her your name again. If an assignment received less than an A, ask why, and find out what you need to do to improve the next assignment.

9   Yes, your professor is busy. So are you. So are your parents who are working to pay or help with your tuition. Ask early what you need to do if you feel you are starting to get into academic trouble. Do not wait until you are failing.

10   *Understand that there will be professors who do not like you;* there may even be professors who are racist or sexist or both. You must discriminate among your professors to see who will give you the help you need. You may not simply say, "They are all against me." They aren't. They mostly don't care. Since you are the one who wants to be educated, find the people who want to help.

11   *Don't defeat yourself.* Cultivate your friends. Know your enemies. You cannot undo hundreds of years of prejudicial thinking. Think for yourself and speak up. Raise your hand in class. Say what you believe no matter how awkward you may think it sounds. You will improve in your articulation and confidence.

12   *Participate in some campus activity.* Join the newspaper staff. Run for office. Join a dorm council. Do something that involves you on campus. You are going to be there for four years, so let your presence be known, if not felt.

13   You will inevitably run into some white classmates who are troubling because they often say stupid things, ask stupid questions—and expect an answer. Here are some comebacks to some of the most common inquiries and comments:

14   **Q:** What's it like to grow up in a ghetto?
A: I don't know.

15   **Q:** (from the teacher): Can you give us the Black perspective on Toni Morrison[1], Huck Finn[2], slavery, Martin Luther King, Jr., and others? **A:** I can give you *my* perspective. (Do not take the burden of 22 million people on your shoulders. Remind everyone that you are an individual, and don't speak for the race or any other individual within it.)

16   **Q:** Why do all the Black people sit together in the dining hall? **A:** Why do all the white students sit together?

17   **Q:** Why should there be an African-American studies course? **A:** Because white Americans have not adequately studied the contributions of Africans and African-Americans. Both Black and white students need to know our total common history.

18   **Q:** Why are there so many scholarships for "minority" students? **A:** Because they wouldn't give my great-grandparents their forty acres and the mule[3].

19   **Q:** How can whites understand Black history, culture, literature, and so forth? **A:** The same way we understand white history, culture, literature, and so forth. That is why we're in school: to learn.

20   **Q:** Should whites take African-American studies courses? **A:** Of course. We take white-studies courses, though the universities don't call them that.

21   **Comment:** When I see groups of Black people on campus, it's really intimidating. **Comeback:** I understand what you mean. I'm frightened when I see white students congregating.

22   **Comment:** It's not fair. It's easier for you guys to get into college than for other people. **Comeback:** If it's so easy, why aren't there more of us?

23   **Comment:** It's not our fault that America is the way it is. **Comeback:** It's not our fault, either, but both of us have a responsibility to make changes.

---

[1] A Nobel prize-winning African-American author.

[2] Reference to a novel by Mark Twain in which one of the main characters is a slave.

[3] After the Civil War, the Freedman's Bureau of the United States government promised each newly freed male slave forty acres of land and a mule as part of a plan to promote economic independence; very few, if any, ex-slaves received this assistance.

24   It's really very simple. Educational progress is a national concern; education is a private one. Your job is not to educate white people; it is to obtain an education. If you take the racial world on your shoulders, you will not get the job done. Deal with yourself as an individual worthy of respect, and make everyone else deal with you the same way. College is a little like playing grown-up. Practice what you want to be. You have been telling your parents you are grown. Now is your chance to act like it.

Understanding Meaning

1. What point is Giovanni trying to make by giving the three examples that she does in the first paragraph?
2. What explanation does she give for why she, an African American woman, is teaching at a predominantly white university?
3. What is her answer to the question whether it is difficult for an African American student to attend a predominantly white college?
4. Giovanni asks what the difference is between prison and college. What is the difference?
5. What is the italicized list designed to help black college students do?
6. What is the list of questions and answers designed to do?
7. *CRITICAL THINKING.* To what extent would the list of helpful hints apply to any college student, not just African Americans?

Evaluating Strategy

1. What purpose might Giovanni have had in using the list of italicized rules and the question-and-answer/comment-and-comeback format instead of using a traditional paragraph structure for the whole essay?
2. Giovanni does not go into the process part of her essay—the list—until well into the piece. What is her purpose in the paragraphs that come before the list?
3. *BLENDING THE MODES.* Where in the essay does Giovanni make use of examples? Comparison/contrast? Cause and effect?

Appreciating Language

1. How do Giovanni's word choice and sentence structure make her readers feel that she is speaking directly to them?

2. What use does Giovanni make of rhetorical questions (questions to which the author does not necessarily expect an answer)?

3. How does Giovanni approach her subject in such a way as to sound not angry about racism but reasonable in her response to it?

Writing Suggestions

1. Write a paragraph in which you explain whether or not you think Giovanni's list of rules applies to any student hoping to succeed in college, not just African American students.

2. Use the fourth paragraph of Giovanni's piece as a model for writing a paragraph, but start instead with the question, "What's the difference between high school and college?"

3. *COLLABORATIVE WRITING.* As a class activity, brainstorm a list of movies about college life. Have someone write the titles on the board. Circle the ones that have to do with racial issues on a college campus. Discuss what picture of life on a college campus each presents. Can you relate any of them to Giovanni's essay?

9

GARY SOTO

Gary Soto (1952–) is a poet whose work has appeared in many leading journals and who has published several books of poetry. He is a native of Fresno, California, and studied with the poet Philip Levine at Fresno State College. Since 1977, he has taught English and Chicano studies at the University of California at Berkeley.

Like Mexicans

BEFORE YOU READ: *You would hardly think that her family's poverty would be what would make a woman a desirable mate, but that may be exactly what a man who has grown up in poverty himself is looking for.*

TIPS FOR READING: *As you read, consider in what ways this essay is an example of comparison/contrast writing.*

TIPS FOR WRITING: *One possible topic for comparison/contrast writing is how something turned out differently from what you expected it to when you were a child.*

1   My grandmother gave me bad advice and good advice when I was in my early teens. For the bad advice, she said that I should become a barber because they made good money and listened to the radio all day. "Honey, they don't work como burros,"[1] she would say every time I visited her. She made the sound of donkeys braying. "Like that, honey!" For the good advice, she said that I should marry a Mexican girl. "No Okies, hijo"[2]—she would say— "Look, my son. He marry one and they fight every day about I don't know what and I don't know what." For her, everyone who wasn't Mexican, black, or Asian were Okies. The French were Okies, the Italians in suits were Okies. When I asked about Jews, whom I had read about, she asked for a picture. I rode home on my bicycle and returned with a calendar depicting the important races of the world. "Pues si, son Okies tambien!"[3] she said, nodding her head. She waved the calendar away and we went to the living room where she lectured me on the virtues of the Mexican girl: first, she

---

[1]**como burros** like burros
[2]**hijo** son
[3]**Pues si, son Okies tambien** Well, yes, they're Okies too

could cook and, second, she acted like a woman, not a man, in her husband's home. She said she would tell me about a third when I got a little older.

2   I asked my mother about it—becoming a barber and marrying Mexican. She was in the kitchen. Steam curled from a pot of boiling beans, the radio was on, looking as squat as a loaf of bread. "Well, if you want to be a barber— they say they make good money." She slapped a round steak with a knife, her glasses slipping down with each strike. She stopped and looked up. "If you find a good Mexican girl, marry her of course." She returned to slapping the meat and I went to the backyard where my brother and David King were sitting on the lawn feeling the inside of their cheeks.

3   "This is what girls feel like," my brother said, rubbing the inside of his cheek. David put three fingers inside his mouth and scratched. I ignored them and climbed the back fence to see my best friend, Scott, a second-generation Okie. I called him and his mother pointed to the side of the house where his bedroom was, a small aluminum trailer, the kind you gawk at when they're flipped over on the freeway, wheels spinning in the air. I went around to find Scott pitching horseshoes.

4   I picked up a set of rusty ones and joined him. While we played, we talked about school and friends and record albums. The horseshoes scuffed up dirt, sometimes ringing the iron that threw out a meager shadow like a sundial. After three argued-over games, we pulled two oranges apiece from his tree and started down the alley still talking school and friends and record albums. We pulled more oranges from the alley and talked about who we would marry. "No offense, Scott," I said with an orange slice in my mouth, "but I would never marry an Okie." We walked in step, almost touching, with a sled of shadows dragging behind us. "No offense, Gary," Scott said, "but I would *never* marry a Mexican." I looked at him: a fang of orange slice showed from his munching mouth. I didn't think anything of it. He had his girl and I had mine. But our seventh-grade vision was the same: to marry, get jobs, buy cars and maybe a house if we had money left over.

5   We talked about our future lives until, to our surprise, we were on the downtown mall, two miles from home. We bought a bag of popcorn at Penneys and sat on a bench near the fountain watching Mexican and Okie girls pass. "That one's mine," I pointed with my chin when a girl with eyebrows arched into black rainbows ambled by. "She's cute," Scott said about a girl with yellow hair and a mouthful of gum. We dreamed aloud, our chins busy pointing out girls. We agreed that we couldn't wait to become men and lift them onto our laps.

6   But the woman I married was not Mexican but Japanese. It was a surprise to me. For years, I went about wide-eyed in my search for the brown girl in a

white dress at a dance. I searched the playground at the baseball diamond. When the girls raced for grounders, their hair bounced like something that couldn't be caught. When they sat together in the lunchroom, heads pressed together, I knew they were talking about us Mexican guys. I saw them and dreamed them. I threw my face into my pillow, making up sentences that were good as in the movies.

7   But when I was twenty, I fell in love with this other girl who worried my mother, who had my grandmother asking once again to see the calendar of the Important Races of the World. I told her I had thrown it away years before. I took a much-glanced-at snapshot from my wallet. We looked at it together, in silence. Then grandma reclined in her chair, lit a cigarette, and said, "Es pretty." She blew and asked with all her worry pushed up to her forehead: "Chinese?"

8   I was in love and there was no looking back. She was the one. I told my mother who was slapping hamburger into patties. "Well, sure if you want to marry her," she said. But the more I talked, the more concerned she became. Later I began to worry. Was it all a mistake? "Marry a Mexican girl," I heard my mother say in my mind. I heard it at breakfast. I heard it over math problems, between Western Civilization and cultural geography. But then one afternoon while I was hitchhiking home from school, it struck me like a baseball in the back: my mother wanted me to marry someone of my own social class—a poor girl. I considered my fiancée, Carolyn, and she didn't look poor, though I knew she came from a family of farm workers and pull-yourself-up-by-your-bootstraps ranchers. I asked my brother, who was marrying Mexican poor that fall, if I should marry a poor girl. He screamed "Yeah" above his terrible guitar playing in his bedroom. I considered my sister who had married Mexican. Cousins were dating Mexican. Uncles were remarrying poor women. I asked Scott, who was still my best friend, and he said, "She's too good for you, so you better not."

9   I worried about it until Carolyn took me home to meet her parents. We drove in her Plymouth until the houses gave way to farms and ranches and finally her house fifty feet from the highway. When we pulled into the drive, I panicked and begged Carolyn to make a U-turn and go back so we could talk about it over a soda. She pinched my cheek, calling me a "silly boy." I felt better, though, when I got out of the car and saw the house: the chipped paint, a cracked window, boards for a walk to the back door. There were rusting cars near the barn. A tractor with a net of spiderwebs under a mulberry. A field. A bale of barbed wire like children's scribbling leaning against an empty chicken coop. Carolyn took my hand and pulled me to my future mother-in-law who was coming out to greet us.

10   We had lunch: sandwiches, potato chips, and iced tea. Carolyn and her
mother talked mostly about neighbors and the congregation at the Japanese
Methodist Church in West Fresno. Her father, who was in khaki work
clothes excused himself with a wave that was almost a salute and went outside. I heard a truck start, a dog bark, and then the truck rattle away.

11   Carolyn's mother offered another sandwich, but I declined with a shake
of my head and a smile. I looked around when I could, when I was not saying
over and over that I was a college student, hinting that I could take care of her
daughter. I shifted my chair. I saw newspapers piled in corners, dusty cereal
boxes and vinegar bottles in corners. The wallpaper was bubbled from rain
that had come in from a bad roof. Dust. Dust lay on lamp shades and window
sills. These people are just like Mexicans, I thought. Poor people.

12   Carolyn's mother asked me through Carolyn if I would like a *sushi*. A
plate of black and white things were held in front of me. I took one, wide-
eyed, and turned it over like a foreign coin. I was biting into one when I saw
a kitten crawl up the window screen over the sink. I chewed and the kitten
opened its mouth of terror as she crawled higher, wanting in to paw the left-
overs from our plates. I looked at Carolyn who said that the cat was just
showing off. I looked up in time to see it fall. It crawled up, then fell again.

13   We talked for an hour and had apple pie and coffee, slowly. Finally, we
got up with Carolyn taking my hand. Slightly embarrassed, I tried to pull
away but her grip held me. I let her have her way as she led me down the
hallway with her mother right behind me. When I opened the door, I was
startled by a kitten clinging to the screen door, its mouth screaming "cat
food, dog biscuits, *sushi*. . . ." I opened the door and the kitten, still holding
on, whined in the language of hungry animals. When I got into Carolyn's
car, I looked back: the cat was still clinging. I asked Carolyn if it were possibly hungry, but she said the cat was being silly. She started the car, waved
to her mother, and bounced us over the rain-poked drive, patting my thigh
for being her lover baby. Carolyn waved again. I looked back, waving, then
gawking at a window screen where there were now three kittens clawing and
screaming to get in. Like Mexicans, I thought. I remembered the Molinas
and how the cats clung to their screens—cats they shot down with squirt
guns. On the highway, I felt happy, pleased by it all. I patted Carolyn's thigh.
Her people were like Mexicans, only different.

Understanding Meaning

1.   What two pieces of advice did Soto's grandmother give him, one good and
     one bad?

2. Some people are guilty of stereotyping Mexicans. How is Soto's grandmother just as guilty of stereotyping Caucasians?
3. When he is discussing Jews with his grandmother, Soto brings from home a calendar depicting important races of the world. When does she ask him for it once again?
4. Where is Soto's mother each time we see her? What does that suggest about Mexican women?
5. What advice does Soto finally realize his mother is really giving him when she says to marry a Mexican girl?
6. Why is Soto pleased once he visits his Japanese girlfriend's home and meets her parents?
7. *CRITICAL THINKING.* Which do you feel would be a larger obstacle to overcome in a marriage, a difference in social class or a difference in ethnic or national background?

Evaluating Strategy

1. In what ways is this essay an example of comparison/contrast? What is being compared or contrasted?
2. How does Soto hint through the first five paragraphs that money is a consideration for Soto, his family, and his friends in choosing a wife? What suggests that sex appeal is also an important factor?
3. In the scenes with his fiancée, there are hints that the sexual attraction is there. What are the hints that the two will be compatible financially?
4. Is there anything in the essay to suggest that Soto may be naïve in choosing a wife for the reasons that he does?
5. Why is a kitten climbing on a screen significant?

Appreciating Language

1. Although Soto is telling his story from the perspective of adulthood, are there ways that through word choice and actions he reveals his youth and naivete at the time he is describing?
2. Analyze the significance of the title.

Writing Suggestions

1. Write a paragraph in which you explain what you think your family's expectations are (or were) regarding an appropriate marriage partner for you.
2. *COLLABORATIVE WRITING.* In a group, share your responses to Writing Suggestions #1 above to see if there is any pattern in what families' expectations seem to be. List the categories that appear.

10

WILLIAM RASPBERRY

William Raspberry (1935–) was born in Mississippi and began his journalism career as a photographer and reporter for the Indianapolis Recorder *in 1956. In 1962 he began working for the* Washington Post. *He received the Capital Press Club's Journalist of the Year Award in 1965 for his coverage of the Watts riots in Los Angeles. In 1971 Raspberry began an urban affairs column for the* Washington Post *that has been nationally syndicated since 1977. William Raspberry was awarded the Pulitzer Prize for Distinguished Commentary in 1994.*

The Handicap of Definition

BEFORE YOU READ: *How do stereotypes affect the way children see themselves? Would African American young people grow up differently if popular culture associated them with chess and computers rather than basketball and hip-hop?*

TIPS FOR READING: *In this* Washington Post *article Raspberry analyzes the effect that the definition of "blackness" has on African American children. Typically, stereotypes are viewed as limiting definitions that are imposed on people. Raspberry suggests that in many instances young African Americans accept negative stereotypes that limit their opportunities.*

Words to know:

deprivation	lack of
conducive	helpful to
quintessentially	essentially, typically
elocution	way of speaking
sustained	constant
innate	inborn, natural

1   I know all about bad schools, mean politicians, economic deprivation and racism. Still, it occurs to me that one of the heaviest burdens black Americans—and black children in particular—have to bear is the handicap of definition: the question of what it means to be black.

2   Let me explain quickly what I mean. If a basketball fan says that the Boston Celtics' Larry Bird plays "black," the fan intends it—and Bird probably accepts it—as a compliment. Tell pop singer Tom Jones he moves "black" and he might grin in appreciation. Say to Teena Marie or the Average White Band that they sound "black" and they'll thank you.

3   But name one pursuit, aside from athletics, entertainment or sexual performance, in which a white practitioner will feel complimented to be told he does it "black." Tell a white broadcaster he talks "black" and he'll sign up for diction lessons. Tell a white reporter he writes "black" and he'll take a writing course. Tell a white lawyer he reasons "black" and he might sue you for slander.

4   What we have here is a tragically limited definition of blackness, and it isn't only white people who buy it.

5   Think of all the ways black children can put one another down with charges of "whiteness." For many of these children, hard study and hard work are "white." Trying to please a teacher might be criticized as acting "white." Speaking correct English is "white." Scrimping today in the interest of tomorrow's goals is "white." Educational toys and games are "white."

6   An incredible array of habits and attitudes that are conducive to success in business, in academia, in the nonentertainment professions are likely to be thought of as somehow "white." Even economic success, unless it involves such "black" undertakings as numbers banking, is defined as "white."

7   And the results are devastating. I wouldn't deny that blacks often are better entertainers and athletes. My point is the harm that comes from too narrow a definition of what is black.

8   One reason black youngsters tend to do better at basketball, for instance, is that they assume they can learn to do it well, and so they practice constantly to prove themselves right.

9   Wouldn't it be wonderful if we could infect black children with the notion that excellence in math is "black" rather than white, or possibly Chinese? Wouldn't it be of enormous value if we could create the myth that morality, strong families, determination, courage and love of learning are traits brought by slaves from Mother Africa and therefore quintessentially black?

10   There is no doubt in my mind that most black youngsters could develop their mathematical reasoning, their elocution and their attitudes the way they develop their jump shots and their dance steps: by the combination of sustained, enthusiastic practice and the unquestioned belief that they can do it.

11   In one sense, what I am talking about is the importance of developing positive ethnic traditions. Maybe Jews have an innate talent for communication; maybe the Chinese are born with a gift for mathematical reasoning; maybe blacks are naturally blessed with athletic grace. I doubt it. What is at

work, I suspect, is assumption, inculcated early in their lives, that this is a thing our people do well.

12   Unfortunately, many of the things about which blacks make this assumption are things that do not contribute to their career success—except for that handful of the truly gifted who can make it as entertainers and athletes. And many of the things we concede to whites are the things that are essential to economic security.

13   So it is with a number of assumptions black youngsters make about what it is to be a "man": physical aggressiveness, sexual prowess, the refusal to submit to authority. The prisons are full of people who, by this perverted definition, are unmistakably men.

14   But the real problem is not so much that the things defined as "black" are negative. The problem is that the definition is much too narrow.

15   Somehow, we have to make our children understand that they are intelligent, competent people, capable of doing whatever they put their minds to and making it in the American mainstream, not just in a black subculture.

16   What we seem to be doing, instead, is raising up yet another generation of young blacks who will be failures—by definition.

Understanding Meaning

1. What kind of analysis does Raspberry provide?
2. What do readers expect in a personal column? What standards for gathering and studying data do they require?
3. According to Raspberry, how does the definition of "blackness," internalized by many young African Americans, affect their development?
4. *CRITICAL THINKING.* Does Raspberry ignore other definitions of "blackness" encountered by African American children, such as literature by African Americans they read in school and African American politicians they see on television? If so, does it affect his thesis?

Evaluating Strategy

1. Raspberry opens his essay by briefly referring to other burdens hampering the success of African American children. Why is this important?
2. What evidence does Raspberry provide readers to support his views?
3. *BLENDING THE MODES.* How does Raspberry define popular concepts of "blackness"? How does he use comparison to other ethnic groups to illustrate how definitions shape people's self-concept?

Appreciating Language

1. How does Raspberry use connotations to shape his analysis?
2. Raspberry speaks of an idea to "infect" black children and create a "myth" that morality is a "black" value. What is the impact of this language?

Writing Suggestions

1. Look back on your own childhood, and write a brief essay describing how you came to define yourself. Analyze how it helped or hindered your development.
2. Write an essay analyzing how stereotyped attitudes have led women, the elderly, the disabled, or other groups to define themselves.
3. *COLLABORATIVE WRITING.* Working in a group of students, write your own lists of behaviors defined as "black," "white," "Asian," "male," or "female." Discuss these definitions, and then draft a short analysis of your views and experiences.

11

MAYA ANGELOU

Born Marguerite Johnson in Saint Louis, Maya Angelou (1928–) has distinguished her-self as a poet, autobiographer, and public performer. I Know Why the Caged Bird Sings (1970), the first in a series of memoirs, describes her harrowing youth in Arkansas. She has starred in an off-Broadway play, acted in the television mini-series Roots, and directed a feature film. When Bill Clinton was sworn in as president on January 20, 1993, she became only the second poet in American history (after Robert Frost) to read at a presidential inauguration.

Champion of the World

BEFORE YOU READ: *Try to remember a time when you were watching an event in person or on television and you were aware that you were seeing history made right before your eyes.*

TIPS FOR READING: *At a time in American history when sports teams were still racially segregated, Joe Louis inspired pride in African Americans when he defeated white men in the boxing ring. Notice how the people gathered together in a small store in a little town in Arkansas in the 1930s feel that the whole future of African Americans in America depends on the outcome of a boxing match.*

Words to Know:

string-along songs	commercial jingles
clinch	a grip around an opponent's body
assent	approval
their "Master's Voice"	words that for years were printed on RCA phonographs along with a picture of a dog listening to a phonograph, puzzled to hear a human voice coming from a machine
hewers	cutters
ambrosia	in mythology, the food of the gods; anything that tastes or smells delicious

TIPS FOR WRITING: *As you read, notice how Angelou lets her readers know what emotions the people in the store are feeling. How does she make clear why the outcome of the match is so important to them?*

1   The last inch of space was filled, yet people continued to wedge themselves along the walls of the Store. Uncle Willie had turned the radio up to its last notch so that youngsters on the porch wouldn't miss a word. Women sat on kitchen chairs, dining-room chairs, stools, and upturned wooden boxes. Small children and babies perched on every lap available and men leaned on the shelves or on each other.

2   The apprehensive mood was shot through with shafts of gaiety, as a black sky is streaked with lightning.

3   "I ain't worried 'bout this fight. Joe's gonna whip that cracker like it's open season."

4   "He gone whip him till that white boy call him Momma."

5   At last the talking finished and the string-along songs about razor blades were over and the fight began.

6   "A quick jab to the head." In the Store the crowd grunted. "A left to the head and a right and another left." One of the listeners cackled like a hen and was quieted.

7   "They're in a clinch, Louis is trying to fight his way out."

8   Some bitter comedian on the porch said, "That white man don't mind hugging that niggah now, I betcha."

9   "The referee is moving in to break them up, but Louis finally pushed the contender away and it's an uppercut to the chin. The contender is hanging on, now he's backing away. Louis catches him with a short left to the jaw."

10   A tide of murmuring assent poured out the door and into the yard.

11   "Another left and another left. Louis is saving that mighty right . . ." The mutter in the Store had grown into a baby roar and it was pierced by the clang of a bell and the announcer's "That's the bell for round three, ladies and gentlemen."

12   As I pushed my way into the Store I wondered if the announcer gave any thought to the fact that he was addressing as "ladies and gentlemen" all the Negroes around the world who sat sweating and praying, glued to their "Master's voice."

13   There were only a few calls for RC Colas, Dr Peppers, and Hires root beer. The real festivities would begin after the fight. Then even the old Christian ladies who taught their children and tried themselves to practice turning the other check would buy soft drinks, and if the Brown Bomber's victory was a particularly bloody one they would order peanut patties and Baby Ruths also.

14   Bailey and I laid the coins on top of the cash register. Uncle Willie didn't allow us to ring up sales during a fight. It was too noisy and might shake up

the atmosphere. When the gong rang for the next round we pushed through the near-sacred quiet to the herd of children outside.

15   "He's got Louis against the ropes and now it's a left to the body and a right to the ribs. Another right to the body, it looks like it was low . . . Yes, ladies and gentlemen, the referee is signaling but the contender keeps raining the blows on Louis. It's another to the body, and it looks like Louis is going down."

16   My race groaned. It was our people falling. It was another lynching, yet another Black man hanging on a tree. One more woman ambushed and raped. A Black boy whipped and maimed. It was hounds on the trail of a man running through slimy swamps. It was a white woman slapping her maid for being forgetful.

17   The men in the Store stood away from the walls and at attention. Women greedily clutched the babes on their laps while on the porch the shufflings and smiles, flirtings and pinching of a few minutes before were gone. This might be the end of the world. If Joe lost we were back in slavery and beyond help. It would all be true, the accusations that we were lower types of human beings. Only a little higher than apes. True that we were stupid and ugly and lazy and dirty and, unlucky and worst of all, that God Himself hated us and ordained us to be hewers of wood and drawers of water, forever and ever, world without end.

18   We didn't breathe. We didn't hope. We waited.

19   "He's off the ropes, ladies and gentlemen. He's moving towards the center of the ring." There was no time to be relieved. The worst might still happen.

20   "And now it looks like Joe is mad. He's caught Carnera with a left hook to the head and a right to the head. It's a left jab to the body and another left to the head. There's a left cross and a right to the head. The contender's right eye is bleeding and he can't seem to keep his block up. Louis is penetrating every block. The referee is moving in, but Louis sends a left to the body and it's an uppercut to the chin and the contender is dropping. He's on the canvas, ladies and gentlemen."

21   Babies slid to the floor as women stood up and men leaned toward the radio.

22   "Here's the referee. He's counting. One, two, three, four, five, six, seven . . . Is the contender trying to get up again?"

23   All the men in the store shouted, "NO."

24   "—eight, nine, ten." There were a few sounds from the audience, but they seemed to be holding themselves in against tremendous pressure.

25   "The fight is all over, ladies and gentlemen. Let's get the microphone over to the referee . . . Here he is. He's got the Brown Bomber's hand, he's holding it up . . . Here he is . . ."

26   Then the voice, husky and familiar, came to wash over us—"The winnah, and still heavyweight champeen of the world . . . Joe Louis."

27   Champion of the world. A Black boy. Some Black mother's son. He was the strongest man in the world. People drank Coca-Colas like ambrosia and ate candy bars like Christmas. Some of the men went behind the Store and poured white lightning in their soft-drink bottles, and a few of the bigger boys followed them. Those who were not chased away came back blowing their breath in front of themselves like proud smokers.

28   It would take an hour or more before the people would leave the Store and head for home. Those who lived too far had made arrangements to stay in town. It wouldn't do for a Black man and his family to be caught on a lonely country road on a night when Joe Louis had proved that we were the strongest people in the world.

Understanding Meaning

1.   How would you sum up in a single sentence Angelou's thesis statement? What is her purpose in telling this story?
2.   What different moods do the people in the store go through as they gather, listen to the fight, and then leave? What are some of the exact words that she uses to let her readers know what the mood in the store is?
3.   In paragraph 16, when Joe Louis falls in the boxing ring, Angelou says, "It was our people falling." A few sentences later, in paragraph 17, she says, "This might be the end of the world." Why would a single boxing match have that much importance for African Americans in the 1930s?
4.   In the last sentence, Angelou suggests that it would not be safe for an African American family to be traveling on a country road following the fight. Why?
5.   *CRITICAL THINKING.* Listening to the Joe Louis v. Primo Carnera fight drew African Americans together in a sense of community. What events in recent history do you remember that drew members of a group together in a similar way? Did the events you have in mind draw together only members of a single racial or ethnic group? Are there other events that are of such major importance that they draw together people in spite of racial and ethnic differences?

Evaluating Strategy

1.   This narrative tells the story of a boxing match, but it also tells how the people in the store reacted to the match. Notice the paragraphs that tell

what is going on before the match begins and after it is over. How do those paragraphs help Angelou make her point in the essay?

2. Can you find words in the essay that appeal to all five of the senses: sight, hearing, taste, touch, and smell?
3. Angelou's essay is broken up into many short paragraphs. Why are there so many paragraph breaks? Are your narrative essays likely to have so many paragraphs? How does a narrative writer decide when to start a new paragraph?

Appreciating Language

1. In the second paragraph, Angelou uses a simile, or a comparison using "like" or "as" of two things not usually thought of together. "The apprehensive mood was shot through with shafts of gaiety, as a black sky is streaked with lightning." How was Louis's victory like a streak of lightning for African Americans? Lightning can also be dangerous, of course. How does Angelou suggest the danger in the last paragraph?
2. In paragraph 12, why does Angelou find it ironic that the sports announcer uses the term "ladies and gentlemen"?

Writing Suggestions

1. Choose an event from your past when you felt particularly proud or particularly ashamed. Use first person ("I") to tell the story in an essay modeled on Angelou's. Choose an event that took place in a short period of time, and tell only enough background for your readers to understand the context. Remember that your purpose is to tell what happened and also to make clear how it made you feel.
2. Once you have written a draft of your narrative, go back and see where you might add more details that appeal to the senses of your reader.
3. *COLLABORATIVE WRITING.* Exchange your draft with a partner and let him or her point out any places in the story where the facts are not clear. Ask your partner to tell you what he or she thinks your purpose was, and see if that matches what you intended.

12

SANDRA CISNEROS

Sandra Cisneros (1954–) and her six brothers were raised in Chicago by their Mexican father and Mexican-American mother. She received her BA from Loyola University in 1976 and an MFA from the University of Iowa in 1978. She is the author of three books of poetry and two collections of short stories. She has won awards for her writing from the National Endowment for the Arts and the Lannan Foundation and in 1995 was named a MacArthur fellow. Most of her writing is based on her personal experience as a member of an ethnic minority.

Only Daughter

BEFORE YOU READ: *Sandra Cisneros's father thought the only reason for a girl to go to college was to find a husband, and he himself could not read English. Why, in spite of the literary awards that she won, could Cisneros not feel that she had succeeded as a writer until she had his approval?*

TIPS FOR READING: *With the opening reference to a note that she once wrote describing herself to her readers, Cisneros lets us know that a major factor in her becoming a writer was the fact that in her Mexican-American family, she was both the only daughter and only a daughter. In other words, she had less value, at least in her father's eyes, than his six sons. Her father felt that she wasted six years of college because she never found a husband there. What she did find was a profession. Her father recognized her talent only when she finally showed him a story in his language, set in his hometown, about people he knew. She knew that if she could reach him, she could reach a broader, more public audience with her writing.*

Words to Know:

La Virgen de Guadalupe	a vision of the Virgin Mary that appeared to an Aztec man in Mexico in the sixteenth century, leading to the rapid spread of Catholicism
philandering	engaging in passing love affairs
Fellini	an Italian film director
Pedro Infante	a Mexican actor

1   Once, several years ago, when I was just starting out my writing career, I was asked to write my own contributor's note for an anthology I was part of.

I wrote: "I am the only daughter in a family of six sons. *That* explains everything."

2   Well, I've thought about that ever since, and yes, it explains a lot to me, but for the reader's sake I should have written: "I am the only daughter in a *Mexican* family of six sons." Or even: "I am the only daughter of a Mexican father and a Mexican-American mother." Or: "I am the only daughter of a working-class family of nine." All of these had everything to do with who I am today.

3   I was/am the only daughter and *only* a daughter. Being an only daughter in a family of six sons forced me by circumstance to spend a lot of time by myself because my brothers felt it beneath them to play with a *girl* in public. But that aloneness, that loneliness, was good for a would-be writer—it allowed me time to think and think, to imagine, to read and prepare myself.

4   Being only a daughter for my father meant my destiny would lead me to become someone's wife. That's what he believed. But when I was in fifth grade and shared my plans for college with him, I was sure he understood. I remember my father saying, "*Que bueno, mi'ja,* that's good." That meant a lot to me, especially since my brothers thought the idea hilarious. What I didn't realize was that my father thought college was good for girls—for finding a husband. After four years in college and two more in graduate school, and still no husband, my father shakes his head even now and says I wasted all that education.

5   In retrospect, I'm lucky my father believed daughters were meant for husbands. It meant it didn't matter if I majored in something silly like English. After all, I'd find a nice professional eventually, right? This allowed me the liberty to putter about embroidering my little poems and stories without my father interrupting with so much as a "What's that you're writing?"

6   But the truth is, I wanted him to interrupt. I wanted my father to understand what it was I was scribbling, to introduce me as "My only daughter, the writer." Not as "This is my only daughter. She teaches." *El maestra*—teacher. Not even *profesora.*

7   In a sense, everything I have ever written has been for him, to win his approval even though I know my father can't read English words, even though my father's only reading includes the brown-ink *Esto* sports magazines from Mexico City and the bloody *¡Alarma!* magazines that feature yet another sighting of *La Virgen de Guadalupe* on a tortilla or a wife's revenge on her philandering husband by bashing his skull in with a *molcajete* (a kitchen mortar made of volcanic rock). Or the *fotonovelas,* the little picture paperbacks with tragedy and trauma erupting from the characters' mouths in bubbles.

8   My father represents, then, the public majority. A public who is unin-
terested in reading, and yet one whom I am writing about and for, and pri-
vately trying to woo.

9   When we were growing up in Chicago, we moved a lot because of my
father. He suffered periodic bouts of nostalgia. Then we'd have to let go our
flat, store the furniture with mother's relatives, load the station wagon with
baggage and bologna sandwiches, and head south. To Mexico City.

10   We came back, of course. To yet another Chicago flat, another Chicago
neighborhood, another Catholic school. Each time, my father would seek
out the parish priest in order to get a tuition break, and complain or boast:
"I have seven sons."

11   He meant *siete hijos*, seven children, but he translated it as "sons." "I
have seven sons." To anyone who would listen. The Sears Roebuck em-
ployee who sold us the washing machine. The short-order cook where my
father ate his ham-and-eggs breakfasts. "I have seven sons." As if he deserved a medal from the state.

12   My papa. He didn't mean anything by that mistranslation, I'm sure. But
somehow I could feel myself being erased. I'd tug my father's sleeve and
whisper: "Not seven sons. Six! and *one daughter.*"

13   When my oldest brother graduated from medical school, he fulfilled my
father's dream that we study hard and use this—our heads, instead of this—
our hands. Even now my father's hands are thick and yellow, stubbed by a
history of hammer and nails and twine and coils and springs. "Use this," my
father said, tapping his head, "and not this," showing us those hands. He
always looked tired when he said it.

14   Wasn't college an investment? And hadn't I spent all those years in college? And if I didn't marry, what was it all for? Why would anyone go to college
and then choose to be poor? Especially someone who had always been poor.

15   Last year, after ten years of writing professionally, the financial rewards
started to trickle in. My second National Endowment for the Arts Fellow-
ship. A guest professorship at the University of California, Berkeley. My
book, which sold to a major New York publishing house.

16   At Christmas, I flew home to Chicago. The house was throbbing, same as
always; hot *tamales* and sweet *tamales* hissing in my mother's pressure cooker,
and everybody—mother, six brothers, wives, babies, aunts, cousins—talking
too loud and at the same time, like in a Fellini film, because that's just how
we are.

17   I went upstairs to my father's room. One of my stories had just been
translated into Spanish and published in an anthology of Chicano writing,
and I wanted to show it to him. Ever since he recovered from a stroke two

years ago, my father likes to spend his leisure hours horizontally. And that's how I found him, watching a Pedro Infante movie on Galavision and eating rice pudding.

18   There was a glass filmed with milk on the bedside table. There were several vials of pills and balled Kleenex. And on the floor, one black sock and a plastic urinal that I didn't want to look at but looked at anyway. Pedro Infante was about to burst into song, and my father was laughing.

19   I'm not sure if it was because my story was translated into Spanish, or because it was published in Mexico, or perhaps because the story dealt with Tepeyac, the *colonia* my father was raised in, but at any rate, my father punched the mute button on his remote control and read my story.

20   I sat on the bed next to my father and waited. He read it very slowly. As if he were reading each line over and over. He laughed at all the right places and read lines he liked out loud. He pointed and asked questions: "Is this So-and-so?" "Yes," I said. He kept reading.

21   When he was finally finished, after what seemed like hours, my father looked up and asked: "Where can we get more copies of this for the relatives?"

22   Of all the wonderful things that happened to me last year, that was the most wonderful.

Understanding Meaning

1. There are cultures in the world in which women are viewed as having little value. An old Chinese saying claims that "geese are better than girls." Cisneros's Mexican father may not go that far, but she says that she felt like she was being erased each time her father referred to his seven *sons* instead of his seven *children*. Why does he look upon her as his only daughter, but also as *only* a daughter?

2. Cisneros and her father agree that Cisneros should go to college, but they have different reasons. What are those reasons?

3. Why does Cisneros feel that it is so important for her to win her father's approval of her writing? After all, she had won literary awards before he ever read one of her stories.

4. What difference does it make that not only is the story she shows him written in Spanish but also that it refers to people and places that he knows?

Evaluating Strategy

1. Cisneros tells us that she described herself once as "the only daughter in a family of six sons." In paragraph 2 she lists different ways she could have described herself. How does each tell us something different about her? Why is it important that she starts paragraph 3 with the one that she feels is most accurate: "I was/am the only daughter and *only* a daughter"?
2. *BLENDING THE MODES.* Some narratives cover a very short period of time. Cisneros's gives a lot of background that leads up to the scene where her father finally reads one of her stories. What sort of information is Cisneros providing that helps make clear why her father's response to her story was so important to her?

Appreciating Language

1. How is it typical of Cisneros's father that he introduces her as "el maestro" ("teacher") instead of "profesora" ("professor") (paragraph 6)?
2. Why would her father mistranslate "siete hijos" ("seven children") as "seven sons"? Notice Cisneros's response: "Somehow I could feel myself being erased" (paragraphs 11–12).

Writing Suggestions

1. *PREWRITING.* How did your parents or other family members feel about your attending college? Was it something expected of you? Was it a decision that some members of your family did not agree with? What other reactions did they have?
2. Write a paragraph in which you recall a time when someone close to you recognized a talent or characteristic of yours that had gone unnoticed before. Make clear how that recognition made you feel.
3. *COLLABORATIVE WRITING.* Discuss with your group whether or not you think there is discrimination against women in education today. Are there majors, for instance, where most of the students are male? Why? Is the same true of women in other majors? Why?

13

SOJOURNER TRUTH

Sojourner Truth (c.1797—1883) was given the name Isabella when she was born into slavery in New York and was sold three times before she was twelve. She escaped in 1827, one year before slavery was abolished in New York, and in 1843 took the name Sojourner after she had a mystical vision. Although illiterate, she became an outspoken and popular lecturer on the subject of abolition and, after the Civil War, on the subject of women's suffrage. She died in 1883 in Michigan.

Ain't I a Woman?

BEFORE YOU READ: *The women's rights movement of the 1960s and 1970s forced our nation to rethink women's roles and rights. In this brief speech given at a women's rights convention in 1851, over a hundred years earlier, Sojourner Truth raised the question of what exactly it means to be a woman.*

TIPS FOR READING: *Keep in mind that you are reading a speech recorded by an observer. As she spoke, Truth did not have in mind a print audience. Her speech may not be grammatically correct, but it captures her passion for her subject.*

TIPS FOR WRITING: *Generally you will not make use of dialect in your writing, but you may do so at times if you are trying to capture realistic dialogue.*

1   Well, children, where there is so much racket there must be something out of kilter. I think that 'twixt the negroes of the South and the women at the North, all talking about rights, the white men will be in a fix pretty soon. But what's all this here talking about?

2   That man over there says that women need to be helped into carriages, and lifted over ditches, and to have the best place everywhere. Nobody ever helps me into carriages, or over mudpuddles, or gives me any best place! And ain't I a woman? Look at me! Look at my arm! I have ploughed and planted, and gathered into barns, and no man could head me! And ain't I a woman? I could work as much and eat as much as a man—when I could get it—and bear the lash as well! And ain't I a woman? I have borne thirteen children, and seen them most all sold off to slavery, and when I cried out with my mother's grief, none but Jesus heard me! And ain't I a woman?

3   Then they talk about this thing in the head; what's this they call it? [Intellect, someone whispers.] That's it, honey. What's that got to do with women's rights or negro's rights? If my cup won't hold but a pint, and yours

holds a quart, wouldn't you be mean not to let me have my little half-measure full?

4   Then that little man in black there, he says women can't have as much rights as men, 'cause Christ wasn't a woman! Where did your Christ come from? Where did your Christ come from? From God and a woman! Man had nothing to do with Him.

5   If the first woman God ever made was strong enough to turn the world upside down all alone, these women together ought to be able to turn it back, and get it right side up again! And now they is asking to do it, the men better let them.

6   Obliged to you for hearing on me, and now old Sojourner ain't got nothing more to say.

Understanding Meaning

1.   Truth says that white men will soon find themselves in trouble because two groups are talking about their own rights. Which two groups are those?
2.   In paragraphs 2, 3, and 4, Truth gives three different reasons that some people say women should not have rights equal to those of men. What are the three reasons, and how does Truth argue against each?
3.   What details about her life as a slave does Truth reveal in this short passage?
4.   Truth does not offer a simple one-sentence definition of what a woman is. In your opinion, how would she define the term "woman"?
5.   *CRITICAL THINKING.* Sojourner Truth was illiterate. Would you agree that in spite of that, she was wise? Explain.

Evaluating Strategy

1.   Truth's speech did not originally have a title. The title usually given it is "Ain't I a Woman?" because Truth repeats that question several times. What is the effect of that repeated question?
2.   Sometimes it might weaken an argument to sum up your opponent's point of view. Does it weaken Truth's argument for her to bring up the other side of the argument with such statements as "That man over there says . . . ," "Then they talk about . . . ," and "Then that little man in black there, he says . . ."? Explain.
3.   Truth ends by stating, "and now old Sojourner ain't got nothing more to say." Has she said enough to build a convincing case? What is the effect of her ending by referring to herself as "old Sojourner"?

Appreciating Language

1. Why would Truth have addressed her audience as "children," and than later one of them as "honey"?
2. What does Truth mean when she says, "If my cup won't hold but a pint, and yours holds a quart, wouldn't you be mean not to let me have my little half-measure full?" (paragraph 3)
3. What biblical allusions does Truth make?

Writing Suggestions

1. *COLLABORATIVE WRITING.* Work with your group to list the different characteristics that, for Truth, define womanhood. Then come up with the group's list of what today defines womanhood. Are the two lists the same?
2. Explain in one to two paragraphs how slavery forced a very different definition of "true womanhood" for black women than for white women.
3. Write an essay in which you argue whether our society has gone too far or not far enough in trying to make men and women equal.

14

THOMAS FRIEDMAN

*Thomas Friedman (1953–) was born in Minneapolis and received a BA in Mediter-
ranean studies from Brandeis University and an MA in Modern Middle East studies
from Oxford. In 1981 he became a reporter for the* New York Times. *In the 1980s
Friedman served as the bureau chief in Beruit and later Jerusalem. He received the
Pulitzer Prize for international reporting in 1983 and 1988. His recent books include*
The Lexus and the Olive Tree: Understanding Globalization *(1999) and* Longitudes
and Attitudes *(2002).*

Because We Could

BEFORE YOU READ: *This article appeared as an op-ed piece in the* New York Times *in
July 2003, after the United States occupied Iraq. Coalition forces found no weapons of mass
destruction, which both the American and British government cited as reasons for the invasion. Friedman argues that the war was very necessary but for very different reasons—the
real reason, the right reason, and the moral reason.*

TIPS FOR READING: *Notice how Friedman uses division to present four reasons for fighting the war in Iraq: the real reason, the right reason, the moral reason, and the stated or
given reason.*

Words to Know:

al-Qaeda	Arabic for "the base," the name of Osama bin Laden's organization
P.R.	public relations
neocons	slang for neo-conservatives who often advocate an aggressive foreign policy

1   The failure of the Bush team to produce any weapons of mass destruction
(W.M.D.'s) in Iraq is becoming a big, big story. But is it the real story we
should be concerned with? No. It was the wrong issue before the war, and
it's the wrong issue now.

2   Why? Because there were actually four reasons for this war: the real reason, the right reason, the moral reason and the stated reason.

3   The "real reason" for this war, which was never stated, was that after 9/11
America needed to hit someone in the Arab-Muslim world. Afghanistan wasn't
enough. Because a terrorism bubble had built up over there—a bubble that

posed a real threat to the open societies of the West and needed to be punctured. This terrorism bubble said that plowing airplanes into the World Trade Center was O.K., having Muslim preachers say it was O.K. was O.K., having state-run newspapers call people who did such things "martyrs" was O.K. and allowing Muslim charities to raise money for such "martyrs" was O.K. Not only was all this seen as O.K., there was a feeling among radical Muslims that suicide bombing would level the balance of power between the Arab world and the West, because we had gone soft and their activists were ready to die.

4   The only way to puncture that bubble was for American soldiers, men and women, to go into the heart of the Arab-Muslim world, house to house, and make clear that we are ready to kill, and to die, to prevent our open society from being undermined by this terrorism bubble. Smashing Saudi Arabia or Syria would have been fine. But we hit Saddam for one simple reason: because we could, and because he deserved it and because he was right in the heart of that world. And don't believe the nonsense that this had no effect. Every neighboring government—and 98 percent of terrorism is about what governments let happen—got the message. If you talk to U.S. soldiers in Iraq they will tell you this is what the war was about.

5   The "right reason" for this war was the need to partner with Iraqis, post-Saddam, to build a progressive Arab regime. Because the real weapons of mass destruction that threaten us were never Saddam's missiles. The real weapons that threaten us are the growing number of angry, humiliated young Arabs and Muslims, who are produced by failed or failing Arab states—young people who hate America more than they love life. Helping to build a decent Iraq as a model for others and solving the Israeli-Palestinian conflict are the necessary steps for defusing the ideas of mass destruction, which are what really threaten us.

6   The "moral reason" for the war was that Saddam's regime was an engine of mass destruction and genocide that had killed thousands of his own people, and neighbors, and needed to be stopped.

7   But because the Bush team never dared to spell out the real reason for the war, and (wrongly) felt that it could never win public or world support for the right reasons and the moral reasons, it opted for the "stated reason": the notion that Saddam had weapons of mass destruction that posed an immediate threat to America. I argued before the war that Saddam posed no such threat to America, and had no links with al-Qaeda, and that we couldn't take the nation to war "on the wings of a lie." I argued that Mr. Bush should fight this war for the right reasons and the moral reasons. But he stuck with this W.M.D. argument for P.R. reasons.

8   Once the war was over and I saw the mass graves and the true extent of Saddam's genocidal evil, my view was that Mr. Bush did not need to find any

W.M.D.'s to justify the war for me. I still feel that way. But I have to admit that I've always been fighting my own war in Iraq. Mr. Bush took the country into his war. And if it turns out that he fabricated the evidence for his war (which I wouldn't conclude yet), that would badly damage America and be a very serious matter.

9   But my ultimate point is this: Finding Iraq's W.M.D.'s is necessary to preserve the credibility of the Bush team, the neocons, Tony Blair and the C.I.A. But rebuilding Iraq is necessary to win the war. I won't feel one whit more secure if we find Saddam's W.M.D.'s, because I never felt he would use them on us. But I will feel terribly insecure if we fail to put Iraq onto a progressive path. Because if that doesn't happen, the terrorism bubble will reinflate and bad things will follow. Mr. Bush's credibility rides on finding W.M.D.'s, but America's future, and the future of the Mideast, rides on our building a different Iraq. We must not forget that.

Understanding Meaning

1. What, in Friedman's view, was the "real reason" for invading Iraq? Why does he believe that "Afghanistan wasn't enough"?
2. What signal, in Friedman's view, did the invasion send to neighboring Arab states? Do you think it will encourage them to suppress terrorist organizations within their borders to prevent hostile American action? Or will it, as the president of Egypt predicted, create a hundred bin Ladens?
3. What in the author's view are the "real weapons of mass destruction"? Do you think it is possible for occupying forces to create a modern progressive nation in Iraq?
4. What significance does the discovery of mass graves in Iraq have for Friedman? How do they shape his view of the war?
5. *CRITICAL THINKING.* Do you think any president can take the United States to war for strictly moral reasons? Does a democracy need to believe it will only wage defensive wars? Could, or should, a future president, in your view, convince Americans to wage a war against a brutal regime if it posed no threat to the United States?

Evaluating Strategy

1. How does Friedman address critics of the war in the opening paragraph?
2. Friedman outlines four reasons for the war. Do you find it effective to number points? Does it help organize a writer's thoughts?
3. How does Friedman support his point of view? What evidence does he provide?

Appreciating Language

1. Does the use of simple words like "OK," "smash," and "bubble" make the article easy to understand, or does it weaken the author's credibility? Can simple language, even slang, be suited to a discussion of serious issues such as war and foreign policy?
2. Consider Friedman's phrase describing Arab young people: "who hate America more than they love life." Do you think this helps to explain suicide bombers?

Writing Suggestions

1. Write a short letter to the editor responding to Friedman's "real reason" for waging the war in Iraq. Do you agree or disagree with his position?
2. *COLLABORATIVE WRITING.* Working with other students, write a short paragraph outlining your group's view about what steps the United States should take in Iraq today. If your group has differing opinions, draft opposing viewpoints.

15

MAHATHIR BIN MOHAMAD

Mahathir bin Mohamad (1925–) was born in Malaysia and was educated at King Edward VII College and Harvard University. He practiced medicine in Malaysia for fifteen years. In 1963 he served as the Malaysian representative to the United Nations. From 1981–2003 he was the Prime Minister of Malaysia.

Terrorism and Islam: Maintaining Our Faith

BEFORE YOU READ: *This is not like most articles you might read. This is the text of a speech delivered in 2002 by the Prime Minister of Malaysia before the Organization of Islamic Countries (OIC), which represents 57 Muslim countries. Prime Minister Mohamad argues that the current plight of Muslims is not the will of Allah or caused by enemies of Islam but is caused by Muslims themselves. Having missed the industrial revolution, the Muslim world is now missing out on the information revolution.*

TIPS FOR READING: *Mohamad addresses a special audience—representatives of Muslim countries. Notice how much of his speech is really a kind of lecture, urging Muslims to stop blaming others for their problems and to examine their own values and attitudes. Consider how difficult it is to challenge people without offending or angering them.*

Words to Know:

ummah	the community of Muslims
adhering	following
implementing	putting into practice
insulate	separate
prowess	skill
secular	nonreligious
infidels	nonbelievers
injunctions	bans
apostates	people who have renounced or abandoned their faith
Jenin	Palestinian town attacked by Israel
acquiring	gaining
diligently	by hard work
jurisprudence	law
obvious	clear
endow	donate or give

"Terrorism and Islam: Maintaining Our Faith" by Mahathir bin Mohamad from VITAL SPEECHES OF THE DAY, June 1, 2002.

zakat	one of the Five Pillars of Islam; donating or pledging
beneficiaries	those receiving aid or charity
alms	donations to the poor
sustain	maintain
inequities	inequalities
implication	suggestion
obligation	requirement

1   I would like to welcome all the delegates to this OIC Conference of the Ministers of Endowments and Islamic Affairs being held here in Kuala Lumpur.

2   *Alhamdullillah* we are grateful to Allah the Almighty for allowing Ministers from Muslim countries to again meet each other at this conference. This conference is only held once every three years, and I am sure there are many issues on the development and welfare of the *ummah* which must be discussed and shared among OIC member countries, so we may better serve the well-being of our people.

3   I am sure you have come here to discuss the religious, economic and social problems of the ummah with open minds and are concerned about adhering to and implementing the true teachings of our religion. I believe that we all have to face the reality of the world of today, a world which has become smaller because of jet travel and real time communication of information, a world in which we the Muslims can no longer isolate and insulate ourselves from each other or the wider world of non-Muslim countries. Whether we like it or not we have to make adjustments to our way of life so as to maintain our faith intact, so as to give meaning to our belief that Islam is for all times and not just for the 1st century of the Hijrah or the 7th century of the Christian era only.

4   For 13 centuries the Islamic civilisation thrived. Muslims were supreme in every field; in the administration and development of their land, in the arts and the sciences, in industry and in trade. The world looked up to the Muslims and respected their military prowess and submitted to their rule. It was an empire that seemed destined to last forever.

5   But we know that it did not. In 1492 the last Muslim ruler of Granada was forced to surrender his country to the Spaniards and retreat to North Africa. In the 1920s the Turkish Muslim empire collapsed due to attacks by Anglo-French forces. Practically the whole of Asia Minor or Turkey as we know it today came under Greek occupation. If it had not been for Mustafa Karnal, the leader many Muslims love to condemn, there would not be any Turkey, secular or otherwise, today.

6   Many Muslims accept the demise of the Muslim Empire as "takdir," as Allah's will. Muslims never really studied the role that they themselves played which brought about their downfall. They never blame themselves. In insisting that it was Allah's will, Muslims are indirectly blaming Allah for their misfortunes. Yet the Al-Quran clearly states that the bad things that happen to us is due to ourselves, the good is from Allah. So how could Allah bring us misfortune? How could Allah be blamed? Surely the people to be blamed for the collapse of the Muslim Empire and the sad plight of the Muslims today are the Muslims themselves. They have done little to save their empire and civilisation, to save themselves from oppression, their religion from being dishonoured.

7   If it is all the will of Allah why do Muslims struggle at all? Why do they explode bombs on their bodies and why do they crash aircrafts against the World Trade Centre and the Pentagon, killing themselves and many innocent people, some of whom are not even their declared enemy. If they believe that this world is for the infidels then they should suffer oppression, indignities and killings and not even struggle against oppression. They should say it is Allah's will and as Muslims they cannot fight what is ordained by Allah.

8   To be very crude the fate of the Muslims today is of their own making. It is not ordained but it is basically because they ignore the true teachings of Islam, the injunctions of the Al-Quran and the guidance of the true Hadith. They quote the Quran often enough but only to explain away their wrong deeds. They can even explain why they as Muslims deny that all Muslims are their brothers as taught by Islam. And having declared certain Muslims are apostates they then kill these Muslims in the name of Islam. The result is that more Muslims are killed by brother Muslims than by the infidel enemies of Islam. The result is that Muslims and Muslim countries are weak and incapable of protecting themselves and their countries. The result is that Muslims live in poverty and misery. The result is Jenin.

9   Islam enjoins upon the Muslims to read, "Iqraq." You cannot read without learning and acquiring knowledge. In the early years of Islam the Muslims applied themselves diligently to reading. They did not read just the Quran and the Hadith but they read the works of the Greek and other ancient scholars and philosophers and elaborated and extended the knowledge that they acquired. The whole scholastic world in those days had to study Arabic in order to learn the teachings of the Greeks and other great scholars of history. Arabic became the language of mathematics, the sciences, philosophy, navigation, etc.

10   Then came those Muslim scholars who condemn knowledge that was not about the religion of Islam. They formulated Islamic jurisprudence

which tolerated no opposition. Islam was all about sins and punishment. All the rest that is enjoined upon Muslims in the Quran and Hadith that was not about sins and punishment were ignored. With the advent of these Muslim jurists and their insistence that the only knowledge that Muslims should acquire was about Islam, the study of science, mathematics, philosophy and other so-called worldly knowledge were ignored. Muslims became more and more ignorant about the world in which they live, about engineering and development, about the advances in industry and the production of goods and services. The weapons of war that they used did not improve and they resorted to buying weapons from others, many of whom were their enemies.

11   They missed the Industrial Revolution completely. And they became client states of the non-Muslims. And now they are going to miss the Information Age, the revolution in communication and knowledge-based economy. They are likely to say that it is the will of Allah that they become even more backward and weak. Yet if they participate actively in the development and application of the new technologies they can become as strong as their detractors. And if that happens surely it will also be the will of Allah. Allah asks us to change ourselves before He will grant us success.

12   It is an important part of the teachings of Islam that we practise charity, that we give alms to the poor, that we endow a part or the whole of our wealth to Islam and the Muslim community. It is obvious that charity requires ownership of wealth in the first place. It is equally obvious that the more wealth and property that we acquire the more we can endow. On the other hand if we are poor there is not much or nothing that we can give as endowment.

13   Yet there is a belief among many Muslims that being rich is sinful. This belief is held despite the Islamic teaching that being poor is close to being *kufur*, being un-Islamic.

14   There is jealousy and hate even of the rich, that somehow they are not good Muslims. Yet Allah has promised that He will raise some above others. In other words we can be either rich, or poor, elevated in stature and power above others without affecting our equality before Allah. We are only better in accordance to our submission or *takwa* before Allah, whether we are high or low, rich or poor. The rich who give to charity because he submits to Allah is as good as anyone else who submits to Allah, who obeys the injunctions of Allah.

15   If we can imagine all members of the Muslim *ummah* as being uniformly poor, then charity would not be possible and the poor cannot benefit from the generosity that is enjoined by Islam upon Muslims. They would

have nothing to give away. That is why it is important for Muslims to work hard to increase their wealth. We must work hard not just as labourers but in everything that we do which will contribute to our wealth. We must work hard to acquire the knowledge and the skills to rise to the highest level in our occupation, in our business and in our industries. And all the time as our income increases we must pay our *zakat*, practise *sedekah*, build schools and mosques and other facilities for the Muslim *ummah* and endow a part of our accumulated wealth to Muslims while we are alive or upon our death.

16   We must do all these systematically and without self-interest in this world if possible. Our motive must be charity and not so as to be hailed by the beneficiaries or the public as practitioners of the teachings of Islam. Allah will know that we have given and given with sincerity and we will, *inshaallah* get our rewards in the *akhirat*.

17   Rather than personally donating directly to the beneficiaries we can just pay *zakat* to the officials appointed to collect the *zakat*. The Governments have provided the Office of Muslim Affairs which is tasked with collecting the *zakat* and administering it. We know to whom *zakat* is due and the proportion to be spent on each. It is the duty of the officers to ensure that each will get the correct allocation. Thus the poverty and the needs of the Muslim *ummah* will be overcome. But the *zakat* is not meant for the able-bodied who are too lazy to work. There is no merit in receiving, only merit in giving. That is the teaching of Islam. And so everyone must try not to depend on charity but to work and earn their own upkeep when possible and then they too can donate and endow and receive merit for themselves in the afterlife.

18   It is sinful for a Muslim society not to strive to develop itself. Allah has showered us with all kinds of resources, not least of which is human resources. We are endowed with a strong body and a brain that can think and solve the problems affecting us. Some of us will depend on our hands and legs to perform numerous tasks and as we employ our limbs Allah will gradually increase our strength and our skills. We can become the finest craftsmen producing delicate works of art like the Moroccans and the Uzbeks. Somehow these skills will be inherited by our children through the generations.

19   It is the same with the brain, the acquisition of knowledge and reasoning skills. With repetition we will acquire great thinking, deductive and reasoning skills. Through the generations we will become cleverer.

20   With these skills we can enrich ourselves and enrich our society. We can produce things and invent things, trade and manufacture. Muslims are great craftsmen and thinkers but for a long time they have stopped improving their production or their thinking. And so they keep on laboriously producing things by hand, one by one. But the Muslim population and others has

increased tremendously. Producing one by one by hand cannot supply the needs of the six billion plus people in the world. Because we do not know how to mass produce good products to meet the demand of a mass market, we have become poor. And because we are poor we are not as able as we should be to give alms and to endow towards the Muslim community.

21   We have not made use of what Allah has endowed us with, the brains and the brawn, and it would seem that we are ungrateful for what He has showered on us. On every occasion we pray for Allah's help but Allah will not help us because we have not helped ourselves. Those who say that it is Allah's will that we are poor have forgotten that the Quran has made it clear and I repeat, that all the bad things that happen to us are our own doing but all the good comes from Allah. If we are poor and oppressed, if we can expect no charity from Muslims who are all poor it is our fault and not Allah's will. If we want to fulfill the Islamic injunction that we be charitable then we must use our brains and brawn to enrich ourselves in order to be able to endow our wealth on the needy among us and to provide the amenities for the performance of what is obligatory (*wajib*) for us as Muslims. Mosques in particular should be endowed by the rich after they have paid their *zakat* and given alms to the poor. But we must also endow institutions of learning, research and development which can contribute to a better life for us and our capacity to defend ourselves.

22   It is clear that the teachings of Islam if followed by the *ummah* would result in an equitable and just society and a rich and powerful one. Islam does not preach absolute equality. The Quran is clear in this matter for Verse 21 Surah Al-Israa' states that Allah will elevate some people above others (in rank and in wealth). But the Quran also requires us to be charitable to the poor and to those below us by distributing our wealth through the *zakat*, alms and endowments. No one is prevented from acquiring wealth and through his own labour no one needs to be poor. But if he is poor despite his efforts to sustain himself then the charity of Muslims will ensure that he gets a share of the wealth earned by others. This Islamic system of managing the inequities in human society is far better than any ideology invented by Man.

23   It is in order that Muslims can acquire *halal* wealth that they must acquire knowledge and the skills necessary to bring success to their enterprises. The quest for knowledge is the first step towards the fulfillment of the Muslim injunction to be charitable and to endow the wealth earned for the well-being of the Muslims and their need for institutions and facilities to perform their ritual and non-ritual obligations as Muslims. The acquisition of knowledge that can contribute to the well-being of the *ummah* is therefore a primary obligation. In addition of course the Muslim *ummah*

would be rich and strong and capable of defending themselves. If today few Muslims can practise charity and they are often so oppressed and harassed by their enemies that they cannot even perform the *solat*, it is because the Muslims are poor in knowledge and skills, are unable to enrich their countries and strengthen them against aggression by their enemies. It is shameful and un-Islamic that all we Muslims can do when the Israelis massacred the Palestinians in Jenin and elsewhere is to appeal to others for pity and for help. Clearly the Muslims have not been doing anything to change their own helplessness and they do not deserve to be helped by Allah. Remember that at Badar the small Muslim force fought against huge odds and Allah came to their help and gave them victory. The Muslim force did not fight because of anger. They did not just want to kill their enemy out of frustration. They fought as a force for Islam and they were victorious.

24   Equipping ourselves with knowledge and skills and using them to enrich ourselves and our countries is therefore the sine qua non of fulfilling the injunction of Islam to be charitable and to endow our wealth for the performance and propagation of our faith. The wealthier we are the more we can endow and the stronger will be the *ummah*.

25   I am ashamed that many among Muslims and non-Muslims have made fun of the OIC saying that it stands for *Oh! I see.* The implication is that we just see and we do nothing. Since its founding the OIC has not been remarkable for the things that it does. Indeed it is seldom that the members of the OIC can see eye to eye and agree on anything that needs to be done. Very often we are not even able to meet. Even the agencies we have created have not been able to deliver.

26   If I may be permitted to say it, we Muslims and our countries are not very Islamic. We cannot even regard each other as brothers. While the enemy is at the door we are busy trying to bring down governments and weakening ourselves in the process. The sad thing is that they do this in the name of Islam. Yet if in the name of Islam we promote Muslim unity and if we act together even our weakness can be overcome.

27   In the pursuit of the teachings of Islam on charity we must at least agree to the process. There is much we can do by ourselves and much more that we can do together.

28   I hope that this Conference of Ministers of Endowments and Islamic Affairs can bring about greater cohesion and understanding of the aim of Islam and Endowment and the way we can fulfill this obligation of our religion. Islam is never wrong but the followers often are wrong in their interpretation and practice of Islam. Remember that the sad plight of the Muslims of today is our own doing, is due to our not really practising Islam.

Understanding Meaning

1. What is Mohamad's main message to the delegates of the OIC conference?
2. Why does Mohamad argue that it is not Allah's will for Muslims to suffer in the modern world?
3. According to Mohamad, why do Muslims live in poverty?
4. Malaysia is a highly industrialized and commercialized nation. How does Mohamad argue that there is nothing sinful about Muslims becoming rich?
5. Why, in Mohamad's view, must Muslim countries develop modern methods of manufacturing and trade?
6. Consider Mohamad's statement about Islamic charity, "There is no merit in receiving, only in giving." Is this meant to be a challenge to poorer Muslim nations, who often resent the wealth of the oil-rich states?
7. *CRITICAL THINKING.* Does this address suggest an important alternative message to that offered by Islamists, who blame all the poverty and oppression of the Muslim world on infidels and imperialists? Why or why not? Could moderate and progressive Asian nations come to be more influential in the Muslim world than the traditional Arab centers of Islamic thought?

Evaluating Strategy

1. How does Mohamad address his audience of delegates from 57 Muslim nations? How much of his speech is a call for his listeners to change their way of thinking?
2. How does Mohamad provide an alternative interpretation of Muslim history, especially in explaining its decline? How does this support his argument for accepting modernity?
3. The OIC conference brings together delegates from oil-rich states such as Bahrain and Kuwait and impoverished countries such as Egypt and Syria. Does this explain why Mohamad addresses the issue of jealousy between rich and poor?

Appreciating Language

1. What tone and style does Mohamad maintain throughout his address? How can a speaker admonish or challenge listeners without insulting or alienating them? Is it likely that many orthodox Muslims would reject Mohamad's moderate approach on principle?
2. Do you detect any words or phrases that play upon bias or conspiracy theories?
3. Mohamad refers to the failure of "really practising Islam." Would many delegates see this as a challenge or an insult? Why?

Writing Suggestions

1. Consider Mohamad's call for Muslims to take responsibility for their own plight. Does this message help refute the concept of a "clash of civilizations"? Write a short statement suggesting how the West can work with moderate Muslim states to help reduce the causes of extremism and terrorism.

2. *COLLABORATIVE WRITING.* Discuss this speech with other students. How does this change their view of Muslims, who are often depicted as fanatics and hostile to Western ways? Have the group work on a brief statement that suggests how the Prime Minister's remarks should be interpreted by Americans concerned about terrorism.

16

A. TARIQ KARIM

A. Tariq Karim is the Ambassador of Bangladesh to the United States.

From Terrorism: Addressing Its Root Causes

BEFORE YOU READ: *Ambassador Karim delivered this speech in May 2002 at a forum called "Islam, 9/11, and U.S. National Security" at the American Council for Study of Islamic Societies at the College of William and Mary in Washington, DC.*

TIPS FOR READING: *Karim uses comparisons to Western events, such as Hitler, WWII, and urban race riots, to explain aspects of the Arab and Muslim world. He outlines the causes for terrorism—poverty, lack of opportunity, and a desire for pride—and possible solutions—better education, political reform, and increased opportunities for women.*

Words to Know:

heinous	monstrous
denigrate	degrade, put down
jihad	"holy struggle" sometimes interpreted as "holy war"
miscreants	troublemakers, scoundrels
inglorious	shameful
specter	ghost
malaise	depression, lethargy, despair
pertinent	important
micro-scale	small-scale
euphemistically	pleasantly or positively referred to (when the usual reference would be negative)
anarchic	lawless, wild
manifestations	signs
mantra	repeated prayer or incantation or frequently repeated word or idea
analogy	comparison
rampant	widespread
exacerbated	made worse
macro scale	large-scale
madrassahs	Muslim religious schools
malleable	easily influenced

"Terrorism: Addressing Its Root Causes" by A. Tariq Karim from VITAL SPEECHES OF THE DAY, May 1, 2002.

despotic	**dictatorial**
indigent	**poor**
seminal	**creating seeds of later development, influential**
inequity	**unfairness**
disparate	**different, unequal**

1   9/11—A defining moment, setting a global agenda. The dastardly terrorist attacks on September 11, on the twin towers of the WTC and on the Pentagon, were not just an assault on America and Americans. They were heinous attacks on the entire world as well, because innocent citizens from many countries other than the United States, were among the casualties . . . indeed, they were an attack on humanity. As a result of those attacks we all stand diminished, not only because of the colossal loss of innocent human lives, but also because they denigrate the core spirit and essential values of a great religion, Islam, in whose name these criminal acts were perpetrated.

2   The 9/11 attacks brought sharply home the realization that terrorism was not just something that happened elsewhere, in distant lands among alien peoples, but that it has assumed global dimensions, with its perpetrators harboring a global agenda.

3   What is terrorism?

4   The *Chambers Twentieth Century Dictionary* (1976 edition) defines it as an "organized system of intimidation." The *Merriam-Webster Collegiate Dictionary* (current edition) defines it as "the systematic use of terror especially as a means of coercion." The word "terror" is derived from Middle English, inspired by middle French, Latin and Greek, from words which mean to frighten, to cause one to tremble or be afraid, or to flee; or to arouse a state of intense fear.

Rationalizing Terrorist Acts as Acts of War

5   Osama bin Laden and his likes have sought to not only legitimize but also glorify their heinous acts against humanity as "jihad" or holy war against western oppression and neo-imperialism. By and large the world has rejected that misguiding assertion, while many Islamic scholars have seriously questioned his loose abuse of the term jihad, which has a totally different connotation and basis. I have dwelt on that subject in a talk elsewhere.

6   If one were to play the devil's advocate here, one would ask the question: is there a line differentiating terrorists from freedom fighters? Have not the early political histories of some of the better known leaders or

statesmen of the last century (ranging from Gandhi, Menachem Begin, Yasser Arafat, and Nelson Mandela) been at one time or other so labeled by the regimes opposing them, and were they not prosecuted, convicted and incarcerated for terrorist acts? The Bengalis of East Pakistan were broadly labeled as "miscreants" and "terrorists" during their struggle for liberation by the West Pakistani authorities in 1971. Does the nobility of the cause justify the adoption of inglorious means, particularly such abominable means as Osama and his al-Qaeda used? Or, to indulge in nitpicking, is there a dividing line between a struggle for self-determination and freedom, and mindless acts of wanton carnage against innocent, unarmed civilian men, women and children, and their homes and work places?

7   To my mind, terrorism is Terrorism (with a capital "T"). It recognizes no caste, creed, religion, race, ethnicity, or physical and political boundaries. It stalks a global theatre. Its specter will haunt us everywhere, in all societies, unless we stand up against it, unitedly, and indict its perpetrators. It is even more important that the world simultaneously addresses the malaise from its roots, otherwise the breeding grounds for terrorists will continue to fester, and spawn more creatures of the likes of Osama. In this context, I find a statement made recently by a well-known American very relevant, and entirely pertinent here:

> The war on terrorism has already dealt a major blow to the personnel, infrastructure, and operations of bin Laden's al-Qaeda network. Just as important, it has burst the bubble of euphoria and sense of invincibility among radical Islamists that arose from the successful jihad against the Soviet occupation of Afghanistan. But it is not yet clear whether the war will ultimately alleviate or merely exacerbate the current tensions in the Muslim world. (From *The Future of Political Islam*, by Graham Fuller, former Vice Chairman of the National Intelligence Council at the CIA, article published in *Foreign Affairs*, March/April 2002.)

Terrorism: From the Micro to the Macro Perspectives

8   Every society, at some point of time in its existence has had to, and I daresay will continue to have to, contend with some form of terrorism. Let me draw upon a very local analogy: even the smallest of local crimes may be described as acts of terrorism in a micro-scale, because they do serve to strike localized fear or terror in the minds of people who are victims of such crime . . . ranging from burglary, assault, rape and attempted murder. On a slightly larger scale, when you have inner-city disturbances, and most cities of the world have

what we euphemistically call "vulnerable" areas, breaking out into organized crimes conducted by mafias or triads or whatever name you give them, that is a form of terrorism. When you have outbursts of frenzied, anarchic rioting and looting by rampaging mobs, that is yet another form of terrorism. What do cities do, when you have crimes generated by inner-city decay? How did Washington deal with its inner-city decay in the second half of the last century, particularly in the 50's, 60's and even 70's? What did Britain do when race riots erupted in some of its major cities, in London and Brixton and elsewhere? Certainly targeting, rounding up and prosecuting the perpetrators of crimes, small or large, to the full extent of the laws of the land were one aspect of the fight. But more importantly, the city fathers had to look deeper, into the causes of such inner-city decay, and address them in order to excise the cancer within society . . . by devising education outreach programs, creating jobs, providing better health care and decent housing, and offering alternative healthy recreational outlets for its youth. For it was found that many of the acts of crime, or acts of transgressions against the laws of the land, were spawned by perceptions of neglect, discrimination and apathy by the authorities to their sub-standard, even sub-human plight. Where inner city revitalization programs were implemented successfully, the crime rate dropped dramatically, as did the underlying tension between different segments of society in those areas.

9   However, not all such crimes are committed by the illiterate, the uneducated or the poor. In many societies, violent crimes emanate from ethnicity or religious persecution. More often than not, the outbreak of ethnic or religious related violence and crime are the results of institutionalized bigotry and its exploitation is by motivated people with a political agenda.

10   On a larger scale: if Hitler were to be viewed as the last century's megaterrorist, what spawned an aberration like him to rise and even be adulated by the society, not illiterate but highly educated, which nurtured him and almost unquestionably accepted him as supreme leader? A close look at the plight of the German people following the Treaty of Versailles, and the subsequent decay of Germany (Europe's inner city in the early 30's and 40's) will give us the answer. It was not only the just war that the Allies waged that won the war against Hitler and Nazism, and Italian and Japanese Fascism. Defeating the Axis powers was only the immediate end goal of the war . . . more important was what the Allies did to restore those "mega inner cities" of Europe and the Far East, by rebuilding institutions, reviving economic development and giving those societies the tools and the means to become the locomotives for growth and development in their respective regions, and even globally. Had that not been addressed, succeeding generations in those regions and the rest

of the world would not have been saved from the scourge of war flaring up again, and again and again. Wherever elsewhere in Europe or Africa or Asia they were not addressed with farsighted vision, we witness today the many new manifestations of "mega inner-city" decay and the explosive reactions following in their wake.

11   Globalization is the mantra of the day. The world today is an ever-growing Mega-City . . . I believe the coinage "global village" is a far too romanticized and inadequate description of it. So like in any city, as understood in the conventional sense, this global Mega-City of ours too has untended and decaying inner cities, and the resultant problems that such inner cities tend to have. Crime of the conventional inner cities is, by this analogy, the new phenomenon of globalized terrorism. The local gang wars are no longer localized. Like the ripples generated on a pond when you throw a stone into its still waters, the ripples of violence radiate in ever-larger concentric circles until they encompass the entire world itself. That is why it is all the more imperative today to address, here and now, not only terrorism per se, in any manifestation from anywhere, but also, more importantly, its root causes. Like criminals, in any city anywhere, those who espouse or perpetrate terrorism must be pursued with the full force and to the full extent of the law, apprehended and brought to justice. It is equally important to ensure that the global Mega-City we live in today does not leave unaddressed the decaying vacuums in the many scattered inner cities of our global Mega-City, where the foot soldiers of terrorism are spawned and terrorists thrive.

12   So what are the root causes of terrorism?

13   Again, I must draw upon the micro-analogy of the conventional city and its problems. What are the circumstances that drive people to a life of lawlessness and crime in any society? In most cases, there exist vast differences in the quality of life available to different segments of that society. More often than not, criminals emerge from those areas where poverty is rampant, educational facilities are inadequate or non-existent, jobs are scarce if at all available, and healthy recreational outlets are not readily available.

14   The problem is further exacerbated if the people of those communities feel that they have no recourse for their voices to be heard, and governance is poor, corrupt and indifferent, and not transparent and accountable. Translated to the macro scale, the analogy would apply to countries with authoritarian and oppressive regimes and the absence of democratic institutions and safety valves. In numerous developed countries, the abject failure of governments to provide to its denizens good and honest governance, good education, adequate health care and sanitation services, decent housing and jobs, combined with the stifling by those inadequate, undemocratic

and repressive governments of the aggrieved voices of their citizens, create
and stoke the cauldrons and breeding grounds of discontent and rage.

15   The terrorists who flew those "kamikaze" missions on hijacked planes
on 9/11 were not uneducated or illiterate people but well-educated, if not
highly educated, with superior technical savvy. The three striking factors
common to all of them were: their ages (in the twenties), the regions they
hailed from (Arab countries with entrenched authoritarian regimes and a
total absence of democracy), and their political leanings (underground but
banned political groupings opposed radically to the existing regimes of
their respective countries). Osama bin Laden is a product not only of the
war against the Soviet occupation of Afghanistan; he is equally, and more
essentially, a product of what he perceives as the political oppressiveness of
his country's regime, and its perceived "toadyism" to the United States and
the West, particularly in the wake of the Gulf War. The establishment of
U.S. bases on Saudi soil created bitter resentment among radical underground groups to which belong Osama bin Laden (the individual as distinguished from the mainstream of his family, which ironically was a part of
the Saudi extended establishment and has excellent personal and business
relations with the U.S.A.). Osama's goals, therefore, are essentially political,
and hatred (of U.S. and Western neo-imperialist societies) is a tool he used
to motivate and manipulate his followers and foot soldiers.

16   Where do the foot soldiers of terrorism come from? From the decaying
inner cities of the world (and here we are contextually talking of the Muslim world's inner cities mainly, but this is not necessarily the exclusive
domain of any single faith, since we have also evidence of terrorism in
other faiths as well). Recall the visual images on TV, of young children,
mostly boys, ages five or above, in "madrassahs" in Pakistan and Afghanistan,
rocking themselves into a hypnotic trance while learning by rote how
to read the Quran in Arabic. These "madrassahs" are religious-based
schools, and where the State (or its government) cannot provide schooling
facilities, these "madrassahs" are the only institutions for alternative education available in such regressive states. The point to note here is: these
young children learn to read the Arabic scripts through recitation, but
they do not learn Arabic as a language. The words and verses they commit
to memory do not by themselves impart any meaning to them. The meaning they assimilate from their teacher, who is therefore in a very powerful
position of using his "interpretative" pulpit as a platform to project his
own personal agenda, if he so chooses to do. Apart from the focus on
learning to recite the Quran by rote in a language totally foreign to
them, no other "secular" subjects are taught in the vast majority of

these institutions. It is from among the graduates of these schools of "neo-jahiliya" that the foot soldiers, or more appropriately, the malleable "cannon fodder" of Osama bin Laden and his likes, the Taliban of Afghanistan, were and are recruited.

17   What priority areas need to be addressed?

18   It is obvious from the foregoing that terrorists are spawned, more often than not, from societies marked by despotic and authoritarian rule, which also tend to go hand in hand with the absence of good governance, lack of accountability and absence of transparency. Usually, lack of good governance results in failure to address the concerns of its people, inability to deliver to them essential services they need for a better standard of life, exacerbating poverty while increasing the gulf between a handful of rich elitists and the vast majority of the indigent and deprived. People tend to respond to the stimuli of their perceptions, and being human as they are, even if a government were to provide every one of its citizens all material comforts and facilities, people who are deprived of a sense of participation in the process of governance will resent this deprivation. Like a pressure cooker without safety valves, such a society will explode, at some point of time. Therefore, one of the foremost areas of priority that needs to be addressed is that of good governance and accountability, in a democratic setup (as opposed to dictatorship and authoritarianism).

19   Governments must accord the highest priority to education, particularly education of women who constitute half of any given society. In developing countries where efforts have been made by governments, in partnership with local and international NGOs, to reach education and economic empowerment to women, such societies have shown remarkable progress. Bangladesh is an outstanding example of a densely populated Muslim-majority country, which has succeeded in establishing a functional democracy after overthrowing the yoke of authoritarianism, has a secular world-view and has made remarkable macroeconomic progress in the last decade. The NGO's in Bangladesh played a seminal role in the transformation of the rural society of Bangladesh, by complementing government programs in education, micro-credit financing and development of micro-enterprises, and providing even health care and other essential services.

20   Where Madrassahs are largely the only alternative vessel for education, it is essential that the curriculum of those "Madrassahs" should be broadened to include secular subjects like mathematics, civics, health sciences, etc., which will serve to temper their natural inclination towards fundamentalism, or radical fanaticism steeped in neojahiliya. Islam as a faith was revealed to the Prophet Muhammad, an Arab, to be propagated among the

Arabs of his times who were steeped in what is historically referred to in Islamic history as the age of "Jahilyia," which means, literally ignorance, but to my mind is an incomplete definition of the term, because ignorance can also be innocent, as in naivete; I would more aptly describe "jahiliya" as "malevolent ignorance."

21   The essential message of the Quran in Arabic is universal and timeless. Indeed, Islam today is the religion not only of the Arabs, but a vast number of people who are non-Arabs and who exponentially outnumber the Arab professors of the faith. Nearly half a billion Muslims reside in South Asia alone (India has 150 million, Pakistan 145 million and Bangladesh 130 million). Indonesia in South East Asia has more Muslims than India. There are sizeable numbers elsewhere in Southeast Asia, China and Africa. Yet the language of its teachings remains Arabic. In other words, most Muslims of the world today are "hostage" to the Arabic language, which is not their native tongue. The analogy to this is the manner in which Christianity of the Middle Ages in Europe was hostage to the bigotry of Catholicism and Latin. The infamous "Inquisition" of that period was analogous to the inquisition of modern-day bigots, whether among the Muslims (the Taliban) or in other faiths (among Christians, Jews, Hindus and others). Christianity, and Europe, was able to shake off the yoke of this dreaded bigotry and the tyranny of the Catholic hierarchy of Rome, only after Christianity's Reformation with the discarding of Latin. Such a reformation has yet to take place in Islam. Tragically, the universal and timeless message of Islam has been kept tethered in a time warp by bigotry today.

22   The world community must also seriously address ethnic and other concerns on a regional and global scale, redressing ingrained and widespread perceptions of inequity or unfair treatment of Muslims. It cannot be denied that there has been an ever-growing perception among Muslims of the Western world (and particularly of America) not being even-handed or fair in their policies involving Islamic societies vis-a-vis others, whether in the Middle East or elsewhere. As I have stated earlier, Osama bin Laden's agenda or end-goal is not merely exhorting hatred of America or the West per se, but more of deriving political capital from stoking a picture of a deliberate policy of injustice and inequity towards the Islamic world being pursued by the United States and the West. Perhaps envy of the progress made by the West is as much a factor in this deep-rooted resentment as the perception of discrimination. Political psychologists need to study this phenomenon more closely.

23   Further stoking this blind rage is the perception of the United States and its Western allies applying what is largely perceived as double standards

in their policies in the Middle East, in their disparate treatment of Jews and Muslim Arabs. Did the United States, by its decision to walk out of the Durban Conference on racism in November last year, along with Israel, add a sort of last straw for radical and fanatic Muslims, unwittingly triggering off the terrorist onslaught? It is a question that begs a rational answer.

24   These perceptions may be unfounded or unjustified according to rationale across the East-West divide here, but the fact is that these perceptions do exist, and will not go away unless addressed, seriously and now. In the meantime, unjust and undemocratic societies will continue to spawn the likes of megalomaniacs like Osama; and such "Osamas" will continue to feed these perceptions, inflating them in the process, to the misguided poor, from amongst whom they will continue to draw a constant stream of foot-soldiers and cannon fodder in the militant pursuit of their political agenda, riding on chariots drawn by the twin horses of hatred and vengeance.

Understanding Meaning

1. How has Osama bin Laden attempted to justify terrorism as an act of war? How have Muslim scholars reacted to this assertion?
2. How does Karim define Osama bin Laden's goal?
3. What does Karim identify as the root causes of terrorism?
4. What role do the religious schools or madrassahs in Pakistan play in the war on terrorism? Why is their reform important?
5. How can the world community respond to the needs of the Muslim world to address some of the causes of terrorism?
6. What lessons can be learned by the way the Allies defeated the Nazis in World War II? What were the immediate and long-term goals of the Allies?
7. *CRITICAL THINKING.* Islam began in the Arab countries and the Koran is written in Arabic. Now that Islam is an international faith, why does Karim believe it must cease considering Arabic as its only language?

Evaluating Strategy

1. In discussing terrorism, Karim compares it to crime, which he sees as terrorism on a small scale. Do you find this comparison effective?
2. Karim argues that international terrorism should be fought the way the British fought the terrorism of urban race riots, by prosecuting perpetuators and addressing underlying causes through jobs and education programs. Do you find this analogy convincing? Would this work on a global scale?

3. Karim is addressing academics interested in Islamic studies. What changes, if any, would you suggest making in the article to address a more general audience?

Appreciating Language

1. How does Karim define "terrorism"? What does he mean when he states "terrorism is Terrorism (with a capital T)"?
2. What does Karim mean by the term "Mega-City"? How does it differ from the popular concept of a "global village"?
3. How does Karim translate "Jahilyia"? Why is this an important term? How has this term been used to propagate a narrow interpretation of Islam?
4. Karim uses the terms "radical" and "fanatic" rather than "fundamentalist" to describe the terrorists. Look these words up in a dictionary. How is a "fanatic" different than a "fundamentalist"?

Writing Suggestions

1. Review Karim's main points about the root causes of terrorism and write a paragraph outlining the role education and school reform can have in reducing the danger of terrorism in the future.
2. *COLLABORATIVE WRITING.* Discuss Karim's article with other students and identify his major suggestions for combating terrorism. Do current American policies seem to address his concerns? Write one to two paragraphs that summarizes your group's opinion.

17

Developing a Thesis

> *Come out with your subject pointed.*
> *Take a stand, make a judgment of*
> *value, make a thesis.*
> Sheridan Baker

WHAT IS A THESIS?

Good writing has a clear purpose. An essay is never "about" something. Whether the topic is global warming, your first job, a high school football coach, or *A Streetcar Named Desire,* your writing should make a point or express an opinion. The *thesis* is a writer's main or controlling idea. A *thesis statement* presents the writer's position in a sentence or two and serves as the document's mission statement. *A thesis is more than a limited or narrowed topic—it expresses a point of view. It is a kind of declaration, summarizing your purpose.*

Topic	Narrowed Topic	Thesis Statement
gun control	handgun ban	*The city's proposed handgun ban will not prevent gang violence.*
computer crime	consumer fraud on Internet	*Consumers will resist shopping on the Web until credit card security is assured.*
campus housing	rehabbing dorms	*Given the demand for more on-campus housing, the fifty-year-old men's dorm should be renovated.*
terrorism	cyberterrorism	*Federal security agencies must take steps to protect the Internet from cyberterrorism.*

Everything you write should have a thesis, not just essays that state an argument about a social or political topic. Without a strong thesis, a narration or description can become a collection of unrelated facts. Although a description may not have a thesis statement you can underline, the writing will have a focus, a purpose, a controlling idea.

ELEMENTS OF A THESIS STATEMENT

Effective thesis statements share common characteristics:

They are generally stated in a single sentence. This statement forms the core of the paper, clearly presenting the writer's point of view. Writing a thesis statement can be a critical part of the prewriting process, helping you move from a list or cluster of ideas to a specific paper. Even if the thesis statement does not appear in your final paper, writing this sentence can help focus your ideas and direct your writing.

Thesis statements express an opinion, not a topic. What distinguishes a thesis statement from a topic is that it does not announce a subject but expresses a viewpoint. The statement "There is a serious shortage of campus parking" describes a problem, but it does not express the writer's opinion. "Shuttle bus service should be expanded to alleviate the campus parking problem" serves as a thesis statement, clearly asserting the writer's position on the subject.

Thesis statements limit the topic. Part of the job of a thesis statement is to focus the paper, limiting the scope of the writer's area of concentration. "Television is bad for children" states an opinion, but the subject is so broad that any essay would probably be limited to a list of superficial observations. A thesis such as "Television action heroes teach children that violence is an acceptable method of resolving conflicts" is limited enough to create a far more engaging paper.

Thesis statements indicate the kind of support to follow. Opinions require proof. "Because of declining enrollment, the cinema course should be canceled" indicates a clear cause-and-effect argument based on factual evidence, leading readers to expect a list of enrollment and budget figures.

Thesis statements often organize supporting material. The thesis statement "Exercise is essential to control weight, prevent disease, and maintain mental health" suggests the body of the paper will be divided into three segments.

Effective thesis statements are precisely worded. Because they express the writer's point of view in a single sentence, thesis statements must be accurately phrased. General terms such as *good, bad, serious, significant* weaken a thesis. Absolute statements can suggest the writer is proposing a panacea. "Deadbolt locks should be installed in all dorm rooms to *prevent crime*" implies that a single mechanism is a foolproof method of eradicating all crime. "Deadbolt locks should be installed in all dorm rooms to *deter break-ins*" is far more specific and easier to support.

LOCATING THE THESIS

To be effective, thesis statements must be strategically placed. The thesis statement does not have to appear in the introduction but can be placed anywhere in the essay:

Placing the thesis at the opening provides the essay with a strong opening, clear direction, and an outline of the supporting evidence. However, if the thesis is controversial, it may be better to open with supporting details and confront readers' objections before formally announcing the thesis. An essay that opens with the statement "We must legalize heroin" might easily be dismissed by people thinking the writer must be naive or insensitive to the pain of addiction, the spread of AIDS, and other social problems stemming from drug abuse. However, if the essay first demonstrated the failure of current policies and argued that addiction should be treated as a medical rather than a legal issue, more readers might be receptive to the writer's call for legalization.

Placing the thesis in the middle of the essay allows the writer to introduce the subject, provide support, raise questions, and guide the reader into accepting a thesis that is then explained or defended. However, placing the thesis somewhere within the essay may weaken its impact because reader attention is strongest at the opening and closing paragraphs. Writers often highlight a thesis statement in the middle of an essay by placing it in its own paragraph or using italics.

Placing the thesis at the end allows the writer to close the essay with a strong statement. Delaying the thesis allows the writer to address reader objections and bias, providing narratives, examples, and statistics to support the conclusion. However, postponing the thesis will disappoint some readers who want a clear answer. Delaying the thesis can suggest to some readers that the writer's position cannot stand on its own and depends on a great deal of qualification.

EXPLICIT, EVOLVING, AND IMPLIED THESES

Although textbooks suggest that every essay should have an easily identifiable thesis statement, a sentence you should be able to locate and underline, this is not always the case. Most writers present explicit thesis statements, while others use a series of sentences to develop their opinions. In some instances, the writer's thesis is not formally stated but only implied.

Explicit Thesis Statements

Alan M. Dershowitz opens his essay "The 'Abuse Excuse' Is Detrimental to the Justice System" with a boldly stated, explicit thesis statement:

> The "abuse excuse"—the legal tactic by which criminal defendants claim a history of abuse as an excuse for violent retaliation—is quickly becoming a license to kill and maim.

Advantages

1. An explicit thesis statement is clear and concise. The writer's purpose is stated directly so that readers will not be confused.
2. An explicit thesis can be used to make a strong opening or closing statement.
3. A concise, strongly worded statement is easily understood, so even a casual reader will quickly grasp the writer's main idea.

Disadvantages

1. Explicit thesis statements can present a narrow interpretation or solution to a complex situation or problem. In many instances a developing or implied thesis gives the writer greater freedom to discuss ideas and address possible objections.
2. Because they are so direct and easily understood, explicit theses can easily alienate readers with differing opinions. A developing thesis allows the writer to explain or qualify his or her opinions.

Explicit theses are best used in writing in the modes of argument and persuasion, comparison, and division and classification.

Evolving Thesis Statements

In "Grant and Lee," Bruce Catton compares the two Civil War generals who met at Appomattox Court House to work out terms for the South's surrender. But instead of stating his thesis in a single sentence, he develops his controlling ideas in a series of statements:

> They were two strong men, these oddly different generals, and they represented the strengths of two conflicting currents that, through them, had come into final collision.

After describing the life and social background of each general, Catton expands his thesis:

> So Grant and Lee were in complete contrast, representing two diametrically opposed elements in American life. Grant was the modern man emerging; beyond him, ready to come on the stage, was the great age of steel and machinery, of crowded cities and a restless burgeoning vitality. Lee might have ridden down from the old age of chivalry, lance in hand, silken banner fluttering over his head. Each man was the perfect champion of his cause, drawing both his strengths and his weaknesses from the people he led.

Catton concludes his essay with a final controlling statement:

> Two great Americans, Grant and Lee—very different, yet under everything very much alike.

Advantages

1. An evolving thesis allows a writer to present readers with a series of controlling ideas, allowing them to absorb a complex opinion point by point.
2. An evolving thesis can be useful in presenting a controversial opinion by slowly convincing readers to accept less threatening ideas first.
3. An evolving thesis can help a writer tailor ideas to suit different situations or contexts. An evolving thesis can also be organized to address separate reader objections.

Disadvantages

1. Because the statements are distributed throughout an essay, they can appear "scattered" and may have less impact than a single direct sentence.

2. Evolving theses can make a writer appear unsure of his or her points, as if
    he or she is reluctant to state an direct opinion.

Evolving thesis statements are best suited for complex or controversial subjects. They
allow the writer to address an issue piece by piece or present a series of arguments.

Implied Thesis Statements

In describing Holcomb, Kansas, Truman Capote supplies a number of facts
and observations without stating a thesis. Although no single sentence can
be isolated as presenting the controlling idea, the description is highly organized and is more than a random collection of details:

> The village of Holcomb stands on the high wheat plains of western Kansas, a
> lonesome area that other Kansans call "out there." Some seventy miles east of
> the Colorado border, the countryside, with its hard blue skies and desert-clear
> air, has an atmosphere that is rather more Far Western than Middle West. The
> local accent is barbed with a prairie twang, a ranch-hand nasalness, and the
> men, many of them, wear narrow frontier trousers, Stetsons, and high-heeled
> boots with pointed toes. The land is flat, and the views are awesomely exten-
> sive; horses, herds of cattle, a white cluster of grain elevators rising as grace-
> fully as Greek temples are visible long before a traveler reaches them.

Having carefully assembled and arranged his observations, Capote allows
the details to speak for themselves and give readers a clear impression of his
subject.

Advantages

1. An implied thesis allows the writer's images and observations to represent
    his or her ideas. Implied thesis statements are common in descriptive and
    narrative writing.
2. An implied thesis does not dictate an opinion but allows readers to develop
    their own responses.
3. An implied thesis does not confront readers with bold assertions but allows
    a writer to slowly unfold controlling ideas.

Disadvantages

1. Writing without an explicitly defined thesis can lead readers to assume
    ideas unintended by the writer. Capote's description of a small town may

provoke both positive and negative responses, depending on the readers' perceptual world.

2. Writing that lacks a clear thesis statement requires careful reading and critical thinking to determine the writer's purpose. A strong thesis sentence at the opening or closing of an essay makes the author's goal very clear.

Implied thesis statements work best when the writer's evidence is so compelling that it does not require an introduction or explanation. Writers also use an implied thesis to challenge readers by posing an idea or presenting a problem without suggesting an interpretation or solution. Although you may not provide a clear thesis statement when writing a description or telling a story, your essay should have a clear purpose, a direction. A thesis statement, though it may not appear on the page, can prevent an essay from becoming a list of random facts or a chain of unrelated events.

STRATEGIES FOR DEVELOPING THESIS STATEMENTS

1. **Develop a thesis statement while planning your essay.** If you cannot state your goal in a sentence or two, you may not have a clear focus regarding your purpose. Even if you decide to use an implied thesis, a clearly worded statement on your outline or top of the page can help keep your writing on track.

2. **Write your thesis statement with your reader in mind.** The goal of writing is not only to express your ideas, but also to share them with others. Choose your words carefully. Be sensitive to your readers' perceptual world. Avoid writing biased or highly opinionated statements that may alienate readers.

3. **Make sure that your thesis statement expresses an opinion.** Don't confuse making an announcement or a factual statement with establishing a thesis. Review the wording of the statement to see if it includes action verbs. Readers should be directed to take action, change their ideas, or alter their behavior.

4. **Determine the best location for your thesis.** If you believe that most of your readers will be receptive to your views, placing the thesis at the opening may be appropriate. If your position is controversial or depends on establishing a clear context of support, delay your thesis by placing it in the middle or at the conclusion.

Continued

5. **Make sure your thesis matches your purpose.** Persuasive arguments demand a strongly worded thesis statement, perhaps one that is restated throughout the essay. If your position is complex, you may wish to develop it by making partial thesis statements throughout the essay. If you are not motivating your readers to take specific action, you may wish to use an implied thesis. State your observations or evidence and permit readers to develop their own conclusions.

6. **Test your thesis.** It is not always easy to find people willing to read a draft of your essay, but you can usually find someone who will listen to a sentence or two. Ask a friend or acquaintance to consider your thesis statement. Is it precise? Does it seem logical? What kind of evidence would be needed to support it? Are there any words or phrases that seem awkward, unclear, or offensive? If your thesis statement seems weak, review your prewriting notes. You may need to further limit your topic or choose a new subject.

7. **Avoid making simple announcements or presenting narrowed topics.** The most common errors writers make in developing thesis statements include simply announcing the subject of a paper or presenting a narrowed topic:

ANNOUNCEMENT:	My paper is about racial profiling. Snowboarding is a popular sport.
NARROWED TOPIC:	Police departments have been accused of racial profiling. Snowboarders are regarded as outlaws by traditional skiers.
IMPROVED THESIS STATEMENTS:	Police departments must develop methods to combat crime and prevent terrorism without resorting to racial profiling. Snowboarders and traditional skiers must learn to respect each other on the slopes.

E-WRITING: Exploring Thesis Statements Online

You can use the Internet to learn more about developing thesis statements.

1. Using a search engine like Alta Vista, Yahoo, or Google, enter "thesis statement" as a term and review the range of sources. You may wish to print out websites you find helpful.

2. Locate one or more newspapers online and scan through a series of recent editorials. Select a few articles on topics you are familiar with and examine the thesis statements. Which sentence summarizes the editorial's main point or assertion? Where is it placed? Are the thesis statements explicit, evolving, or implied? Are they carefully worded?

InfoTrac® College Edition

For additional resources go to InfoTrac College Edition, your online research library, at http://academic.cengage.com/infotrac.

1. Enter the search term "thesis statements" in the Subject Guide or Keyword.

2. Search for online articles about controversial topics such as terrorism, abortion, gun control, affirmative action, privacy, censorship, or a current scandal to locate articles and editorials. Select three or four articles and analyze them:

- What is the article's thesis? Can you restate it in your own words?

- Is the thesis stated in a single sentence or is only implied?

- Where did the author place the thesis? How does its location affect the way people will read the article?

- Does the thesis do more than state an opinion? Does it introduce support, limit the topic, address possible objections?

18

MARTIN GANSBERG

Martin Gansberg (1920–1995) served for forty-three years as a reporter and editor for the New York Times. *Beginning as a night office boy in 1942, Gansberg eventually rose to the position of news editor of the international edition of the* Times *published in Paris. He won an award for excellence from the Newspaper Reporter's Association of New York for the following narrative account of the murder of Catherine Genovese. A resident of the borough of Queens in New York City, Ms. Genovese was stabbed repeatedly by a single assailant during more than half an hour on March 14, 1964, while thirty-eight otherwise decent citizens stood by and did nothing. Although Gansberg was a reporter and editor for decades, he is best remembered for the understated power of this single story.*

Thirty-Eight Who Saw Murder Didn't Call the Police

BEFORE YOU READ: *In your lifetime, you have probably seen hundreds of murders on television and in movies. What would you do if you witnessed one in real life? In his famous article, Gansberg writes about thirty-eight New Yorkers who had to make that decision.*

TIPS FOR READING: *Gansberg organized his newspaper article in such a way that we know the end of the story from the beginning. He tells us in the first few paragraphs how thirty-eight people responded to a neighbor's cries for help and how puzzling their behavior was even to an experienced police inspector. He then goes back to narrate in detail the story of the murder, which took place over more than half an hour. He concludes his essay by letting the witnesses explain in their own words why they did nothing as they heard and saw a young woman being murdered. As you read, notice all the references to time that indicate how much time the neighbors had to call the police before the killer struck the fatal blow.*

Words to Know:	
Queens	a borough of New York City on West Long Island, east of Brooklyn
borough	one of the five administrative units of New York City
staid	sober, settled
Tudor	a style of architecture characterized by rounded arches and extensive paneling

| distraught | very upset, troubled, agitated |
| apprehensive | anxious or fearful about the future |

TIPS FOR WRITING: *Journalists break up their articles into short paragraphs that are eas-*
ier to read than long ones in the narrow columns of a newspaper. As you plan how to break
your narrative up into paragraphs, let natural breaks in the action provide clues as to
where to start new paragraphs.

1   For more than half an hour 38 respectable, law-abiding citizens in Queens
watched a killer stalk and stab a woman in three separate attacks in Kew
Gardens.

2   Twice their chatter and the sudden glow of their bedroom lights inter-
rupted him and frightened him off. Each time he returned, sought her out,
and stabbed her again. Not one person telephoned the police during the
assault; one witness called after the woman was dead.

3   That was two weeks ago today.

4   Still shocked is Assistant Chief Inspector Frederick M. Lussen, in
charge of the borough's detectives and a veteran of 25 years of homicide
investigations. He can give a matter-of-fact recitation on many murders.
But the Kew Gardens slaying baffles him—not because it is a murder, but
because the "good people" failed to call the police.

5   "As we have reconstructed the crime," he said, "the assailant had three
chances to kill this woman during a 35-minute period. He returned twice to
complete the job. If we had been called when he first attacked, the woman
might not be dead now."

6   This is what the police say happened beginning at 3:20 A.M. in the
staid, middle-class, tree-lined Austin Street area:

7   Twenty-eight-year-old Catherine Genovese, who was called Kitty by
almost everyone in the neighborhood, was returning home from her job as
manager of a bar in Hollis. She parked her red Fiat in a lot adjacent to the
Kew Gardens Long Island Rail Road Station, facing Mowbray Place. Like
many residents of the neighborhood, she had parked there day after day
since her arrival from Connecticut a year ago, although the railroad frowns
on the practice.

8   She turned off the lights of her car, locked the door, and started to walk
the 100 feet to the entrance of her apartment at 82–70 Austin Street, which
is in a Tudor building, with stores in the first floor and apartments on the
second.

9   The entrance to the apartment is in the rear of the building because the
front is rented to retail stores. At night the quiet neighborhood is shrouded
in the slumbering darkness that marks most residential areas.

10   Miss Genovese noticed a man at the far end of the lot, near a seven-story apartment house at 82–40 Austin Street. She halted. Then, nervously, she headed up Austin Street toward Lefferts Boulevard, where there is a call box to the 102nd Police Precinct in nearby Richmond Hill.

11   She got as far as a street light in front of a bookstore before the man grabbed her. She screamed. Lights went on in the 10-story apartment house at 82–67 Austin Street, which faces the bookstore. Windows slid open and voices punctuated the early-morning stillness.

12   Miss Genovese screamed: "Oh, my God, he stabbed me! Please help me! Please help me!"

13   From one of the upper windows in the apartment house, a man called down: "Let that girl alone!"

14   The assailant looked up at him, shrugged, and walked down Austin Street toward a white sedan parked a short distance away. Miss Genovese struggled to her feet.

15   Lights went out. The killer returned to Miss Genovese, now trying to make her way around the side of the building by the parking lot to get to her apartment. The assailant stabbed her again.

16   "I'm dying!" she shrieked. "I'm dying!"

17   Windows were opened again, and lights went on in many apartments. The assailant got into his car and drove away. Miss Genovese staggered to her feet. A city bus, 0–10, the Lefferts Boulevard line to Kennedy International Airport, passed. It was 3:35 A.M.

18   The assailant returned. By then, Miss Genovese had crawled to the back of the building, where the freshly painted brown doors to the apartment house held out hope for safety. The killer tried the first door; she wasn't there. At the second door, 82–62 Austin Street, he saw her slumped on the floor at the foot of the stairs. He stabbed her a third time—fatally.

19   It was 3:50 by the time the police received their first call, from a man who was a neighbor of Miss Genovese. In two minutes they were at the scene. The neighbor, a 70-year-old woman, and another woman were the only persons on the street. Nobody else came forward.

20   The man explained that he had called the police after much deliberation. He had phoned a friend in Nassau County for advice and then he had crossed the roof of the building to the apartment of the elderly woman to get her to make the call.

21   "I didn't want to get involved," he sheepishly told police.

22   Six days later, the police arrested Winston Moseley, a 29-year-old business machine operator, and charged him with homicide. Moseley had no previous record. He is married, has two children and owns a home at 133–19

Sutter Avenue, South Ozone Park, Queens. On Wednesday, a court committed him to Kings County Hospital for psychiatric observation.

23   When questioned by the police, Moseley also said that he had slain Mrs. Annie May Johnson, 24, of 146–12 133d Avenue, Jamaica, on Feb. 29 and Barbara Kralik, 15, of 174–17 140th Avenue, Springfield Gardens, last July. In the Kralik case, the police are holding Alvin L. Mitchell, who is said to have confessed to that slaying.

24   The police stressed how simple it would have been to have gotten in touch with them. "A phone call," said one of the detectives, "would have done it." The police may be reached by dialing "0" for operator or SPring 7–3100.

25   Today witnesses from the neighborhood, which is made up of one-family homes in the $35,000 to $60,000 range with the exception of the two apartment houses near the railroad station, find it difficult to explain why they didn't call the police.

26   A housewife, knowingly if quite casually, said, "We thought it was a lovers' quarrel." A husband and wife both said, "Frankly, we were afraid." They seemed aware of the fact that events might have been different. A distraught woman, wiping her hands in her apron, said, "I didn't want my husband to get involved."

27   One couple, now willing to talk about that night, said they heard the first screams. The husband looked thoughtfully at the bookstore where the killer first grabbed Miss Genovese.

28   "We went to the window to see what was happening," he said, "but the light from our bedroom made it difficult to see the street." The wife, still apprehensive, added: "I put out the light and we were able to see better."

29   Asked why they hadn't called the police, she shrugged and replied: "I don't know."

30   A man peeked out from a slight opening in the doorway to his apartment and rattled off an account of the killer's second attack. Why hadn't he called the police at the time? "I was tired," he said without emotion. "I went back to bed."

31   It was 4:25 A.M. when the ambulance arrived to take the body of Miss Genovese. It drove off. "Then," a solemn police detective said, "the people came out."

Understanding Meaning

1. What do you think Gansberg's purpose was in writing this article? Is he primarily concerned with criticizing the thirty-eight witnesses who did nothing?

2. This article has been reprinted hundreds of times since it was first published in 1964. Why do you think this particular article about this particular murder stands out among all the writing about murders that have taken place in our country since 1964?

3. What excuses did the witnesses offer for not calling the police?

4. *CRITICAL THINKING.* Do you think it more likely or less likely that neighbors would ignore a neighbor's cries for help today than in 1964? Explain. Have you read or heard about similar events more recent than the murder of Genovese?

Evaluating Strategy

1. Journalists know that they must place the essential facts of a story in the first paragraph since some readers will not take time to read the whole article. When you write your own narrative, do you think it is a good idea to summarize the whole story in the first paragraph? Why or why not?

2. What effect do you think Gansberg is trying to achieve by mentioning the time so often in his article?

3. Look back at Gansberg's use of quotes. Do the quotes make the article a better piece of writing than it would be without them? Explain.

Appreciating Language

1. In the first sentence, Gansberg refers to "38 respectable, law-abiding citizens." Do you think that he intends to be sincere or ironic when he uses the adjectives "respectable" and "law-abiding"?

2. Gansberg describes the neighborhood in which Genovese lived as "the staid, middle-class, tree-lined Austin Street area" (paragraph 6). Even if you don't know anything about the Austin Street area of Queens, what do adjectives like "staid," "middle-class," and "tree-lined" suggest about this crime and about crimes in general?

Writing Suggestions

1. *COLLABORATIVE WRITING.* Brainstorm with your group about how common crime is (or isn't) in your hometown(s). If citizens in your neighborhood saw something like the murder of Kitty Genovese beginning, what do you think they would do? Do the answers vary according to the

different neighborhoods, towns, cities, or regions of the country the members of your group are from?

2. Sum up in one sentence an idea that came out of your group discussion and use that as the topic sentence for a paragraph. Use examples from your own experience and that of your group members to support that topic sentence.

3. Pretend that you were one of the neighbors who witnessed the murder. In your own words, in one or two paragraphs, explain what you saw and heard and why you didn't call the police.